Mystical Experience and Religions Doctrine

Religion and Reason 26

Method and Theory in the Study and Interpretation of Religion

MOUTON PUBLISHERS · BERLIN · NEW YORK · AMSTERDAM

Mystical Experience and Religious Doctrine

An Investigation of the Study of Mysticism in World Religions

PHILIP C. ALMOND
Universität of Queensland

MOUTON PUBLISHERS · BERLIN · NEW YORK · AMSTERDAM

ISBN 90 279 3160 7

Printing: Druckerei Hildebrand, Berlin. - Binding: Lüderitz & Bauer Buchgewerbe
GmbH, Berlin. Printed in Germany.

To Brenda

This book is intended as a contribution to the discussion of the problem of the relationship between mystical experience and the doctrines of the major world religions. Its general aim is to examine the most important accounts of this relationship offered in the English language during the past twenty or so years. The significance of these accounts lies in the fact that they attempt to resolve the problem of the incompatibility between religious doctrines by appeal to religious experience in general and mystical experience in particular; the philosophical evaluation of the truth of religious doctrines takes place within the context of the description and classification of various types of religious experience.

The first specific aim of this study is then to demonstrate that various views of the relationship between the doctrines of the major world religions depend upon the nature of the respective descriptions and classifications of mystical experience in particular. Thus, the question of the relationship between religious doctrines devolves upon the problem of the appropriate method by means of which mystical experiences can be described and classified. And consequently, the second specific aim of this study is to establish a theoretically cogent conceptual framework for the description and classification of mystical experiences. In the light of this we may hope to arrive at a clearer appreciation of the relationship between mystical experience and doctrinal formulation, and provide a further impetus to the study of mysticism in world religions.

Although the substance of my argument differs from that of Professor Ninian Smart, my indebtedness to his thought and writings is evident throughout. My gratitude is also due to Mr. John Gill of the University of Adelaide; I have profited enormously from his encouragement and advice. My thanks are due too to Dr. Michael Bradley and Dunstan McKee S.S.M. for reading and commenting upon earlier drafts of the manuscript; and to Professor James Horne and Dr. Harold Turner who corresponded with me on a number of issues relevant to the concerns of this volume. My colleagues Dr. Barry Reay and Mr. Gunther Kress have helped me to iron out a number of stylistic inadequacies. Finally, I wish to express my appreciation to Dr. J. D. J. Waardenburg for a number of most important and helpful editorial suggestions. This book is dedicated to my wife in gratitude for her having lived not only with me but also with this study.

Contents

Introduction

Contemporary Western culture has witnessed an ever-increasing growth of interest in the study of the great religious traditions of the world. The present time, showing as it does the collapse of cultural barriers and an incipient revolt against cultural tribalism, together with the fore-shadowed development in Western man of a more global consciousness, is perhaps the most propitious of all periods for the study of world religions.

This situation has arisen, somewhat paradoxically, from that process in Western societies that has been called 'secularization'. On the one hand, Western man in becoming more secularized, in becoming very much the child of the scientific and technological revolutions of the past several centuries, has freed himself from the dominance which religious belief and its institutions — with a predominantly Christian ambience — have had over him. Yet, on the other hand, because secularization has liberated Western man from viewing his world through Christian-coloured spectacles, this very fact has made possible an approach to and an understanding of those spiritual universes within which the peoples of the East have for millenia found their meaning, and by means of which they have mapped out their life journeys.

This is of course not to deny that the phenomenon of secularization is making its presence felt in non-Western cultures. As Paul Tillich (1963:5; see also Benz 1965; Ling 1961) has pointed out,

... the main characteristic of the present encounter of the world religions is their encounter with the quasi-religions of our time. Even the mutual relations of the religions proper are decisively influenced by the encounter of each of them with secularism, or one or more of the quasi-religions which are based on secularism.

Moreover, to some degree, this ideological assault of the West upon the East has brought about a resurgence in Eastern religions, and a reassertion of their autonomy and validity. Still, as K. M. Pannikar notes (1969:329), that these religions are stronger today,

does not mean that they have not undergone profound changes. As against other religions and other philosophies they have more than held their own; but they have also had to undergo subtle transformations to resolve the conflicts which modern science, more than rival religions, forced on them. Thus the new interpretations of Buddhism and Hinduism reflect in a large measure the influence of modern ideas, mostly arising from contact with Europe.

Granted the impact of secularist modes of thought upon the East, it is nevertheless necessary to deny that the process of cultural influence is a purely one-sided affair, that East meets West only in the conflict of the latter's materialism with the former's spirituality. On the contrary, the 'spiritual' gap created by the virtual demise of the Christian scheme of ordering reality has opened up the possibility for Western man to take into his own understanding of the world any one of a variety of Eastern modes of spirituality, a possibility being realized in the Western context. To be sure, this is not to fore-shadow the prospect of large-scale conversion to Eastern norms; but it is, at least, to register the presence of, awareness of, and interest in these norms within the West. Such an awareness is already leading to Western reflection upon the nature of its own religious heritage (Hick 1977a, 1980), to attempts to enrich Western Christianity by an absorption of Eastern spiritual values (see, for example, Moffitt 1973; Johnston 1977; Merton 1961; and Griffiths 1978), or at the very least to a recognition by Christianity that elements of religious truth may be enshrined within Eastern traditions (for a classic account, see Troeltsch 1972; for a Roman Catholic position, see Küng 1967; for a neo-Orthodox Protestant view, Kraemer 1956; see also Hick and Hebblethwaite 1980). Pluralism, indeed the endorsement of pluralism, has become a fact of Western religious life.

This study is devoted to the analysis of a cluster of related issues that arise from the fact of religious pluralism. The issues with

which we are concerned may initially be clarified by asking two
questions. Firstly, granting the fact of religious pluralism, are the (1)
doctrinal statements of the major world religions essentially saying the same thing, or are they totally (or perhaps only partially)
incompatible with each other? Secondly, to which criterion (or (2)
criteria) are we to appeal in order to answer the first question?

The first question, or rather, set of questions, revolves around
what has come to be called 'the conflicting truth claims problem'.
John Hick summarizes it in this way (1974b:140):

The 'conflicting truth claims' problem is just that the religions seem to say
different and incompatible things about the nature of ultimate reality, about the
modes of divine activity, and about the nature and destiny of man. Is the divine
nature personal or impersonal? Does deity become incarnate in the world? Are
human beings born again and again on earth? Is the Bible, or the Qur'ān, or
the Bhagavad-Gītā the word of God? If what Christianity says in answer to these
questions is true, must not what Hinduism says be to a large extent false? If what
Buddhism says is true, must not what Islam says be largely false?

In short, in so far as religions make propositional claims, hold
particular views as to the way things are, such claims and views
are incompatible. (For the fullest account of the logic underlying
conflicting religious truth claims, see Christian 1972.)

The problem thus generated has led to attempts both to resolve
and to dissolve it. Our attention in this study will be focused on
attempts to resolve the problem of conflicting religious truth
claims. But before doing this, it may be fruitful to outline briefly
three ways in which the problem has been putatively dissolved for,
in so doing, we may throw some preliminary light on the nature
of resolutions of the problem.

Firstly then, it has been argued, by Wilfred Cantwell Smith   A
(1959:31–58; 1967) for example, that the notion of religions as
mutually exclusive entities is an illicit reification. Accordingly, he
wants to argue, truth and falsity are not primarily properties of
religious statements or propositions but are properties of persons.
Secondly, the problem may be putatively dissolved by an extreme   B
conceptual fideism in which, because each religion establishes its

own criteria of truth and falsity, there cannot (*logically* cannot) be conflicting truth claims *between* religions. Religious truth is relative to religious traditions (see, for example, Phillips 1976; Almond 1977:218-221; Richards 1980:44-66; and my reply, Almond 1981:178-180). A third way of dissolving the problem is by the denial of factual significance to any (and therefore to *all*) religious truth claims because they are empirically unverifiable and unfalsifiable. And allied to this is the claim that religious statements which appear to be making truth claims are, in effect, merely expressing or evoking emotions, evincing or prescribing modes of action, or merely describing certain kinds of attitudes towards life (see, for example, Ayer 1970; Martin 1959; Hepburn 1958; and Braithwaite 1971).

This is not the place to attempt a refutation of these various attempted dissolutions. But it can be pointed out that, in spite of their very different natures, they are nonetheless unified by their implicit conviction that the problem of conflicting truth claims between religions is a pseudo one that only arises because of a misunderstanding of the nature of religious truth. This study, in contrast, proceeds from the presupposition that the problem of conflicting religious truth claims is a real problem and, in the context of ever-increasing pluralism, a pressing one. The claim that it is a real and not a pseudo problem is grounded on a number of premisses.

Firstly, it is grounded on the premiss that religious statements are serious candidates for truth. Thus, those challenges to religious belief which deny its factual significance in an *a priori* way are methodologically suspended. This is not to assume that there are true religious statements; but it is to insist that judgements on the factual significance of religious statements prior to a thorough investigation of the possible criteria of religious truth are premature. Connected with this is a further premiss. This is to the effect that no particular doctrine or set of doctrines has a monopoly on religious truth. In other words, not only are religious statements candidates for religious truth, but they are *equally* so. Thus, no religious doctrine or set of doctrines can be assumed as normative for the evaluation of the truth status of other doctrines or sets of doctrines.

In addition, the claim that it is a real problem rests on the assumption that the possible truths to which religious statements aver are so independently of the cultural context in which they are made. To take religious truth claims seriously entails the affirmation that if there is religious truth it is the same, so to say, on both sides of the Bosphorus. Finally, this study recognizes that the notion of religious truth *is* intimately linked to the life of the individual believer. But far from dissolving the problem, as Cantwell Smith implies, this fact throws it into stark relief. For the problem of conflicting religious truth claims brings into focus not only conflicting systems of religious metaphysics, but also whole patterns of conflicting religious ways of living.

Having outlined the premises upon which the conflicting truth claims problem is constituted as a real one, we can now turn to the second question adverted to above, namely, to which criterion are we to appeal as a means of resolving it? This study intends to focus on the nature and validity of the appeal to religious experience, and more especially the mystical experience, as a criterion appropriate to this end.

On the face of it, an appeal to religious experience as a criterion of religious truth is a promising line of enquiry. Experience of the transcendent is common to all religious traditions. It is from such experience that all the more general manifestations of man's religious behaviour are primarily derived. And it is to the 'sacredly Real' apprehended within such experience that the more general manifestations of man's religious behaviour are intricately related. There is therefore a universality about religious experience which transcends its various expressions — doctrinal, ritual, ethical, and so on. Religious experience also seems to provide the crucial point of connection between religious doctrines and their transcendent referent. It thus provides a common point of reference to which a variety of incompatible truth claims may be referred.

Consequently, the validity of the appeal to religious experience as a criterion of religious truth is dependent upon two factors. It is dependent on the nature of religious experience; and it is dependent on the nature of the relationship between religious experience and its interpretation in the propositional formulations of the major world religions. In short, the appeal to religious experience is ineluctably connected with the task of the description and classification of religious experience, and the methodology appropriate to this.

This volume proceeds therefore on two broad fronts. On the one hand, we will critically examine attempts to resolve the problem of conflicting religious truth claims by appeal to religious experience. On the other hand, in order to examine the validity of this appeal, we need to come to terms with problems involved in the description and classification of religious experience. More precisely, our task will be to demonstrate that attempts to determine the nature of religious experience are crucially dependent on particular views of the relationship between religious experience and its interpretation in world religions.

With regard to the procedure to be adopted for this latter task, some points of clarification are essential. It would be presumptuous in a volume of this size to attempt to deal with the question of the description and classification of all forms of religious experience. It is necessary therefore to limit the data with which we have to deal; and we will focus, in the main, on mystical experience. This is naturally not to deny the importance of other kinds of religious experience to the formation of religious doctrine. Nor does it preclude our referring to other forms of religious experience in so far as they are relevant to the analysis of mystical experience. Mystical experience falls within the category of religious experience in general and it is to be hoped that such light as is cast on mystical experience will bear on the analysis of other kinds of religious experience yet to receive adequate philosophical treatment.

Our examination of mystical experience is not primarily an empirical one. Rather, it is a necessary preliminary to the empirical study of mysticism (although a number of empirical results will accrue as we proceed). The empirical study of mysticism can only proceed on sound methodological principles established by a thorough study of the possible relationships which may hold between religious doctrines and the mystical experiences to which they are intimately and irreducibly related. The establishment of a conceptual framework within which the empirical study of mysticism can proceed is therefore a crucial part of our study. And the development of such a framework will necessarily have analogies to frameworks pertinent to the study of other forms of religious experience.

But how is the term 'mystical experience' to be used? For reasons that will become clearer as we proceed, it is inopportune to attempt too detailed a description at this point. The meaning of 'mystical experience' for those authors whom we are to examine is very much an outcome of their various views as to the relationship between mystical experience and its interpretation. Still, this much can be said. Most would agree that the term is appropriate for two particular classes of experience. Firstly, we have experiences in which the world of every-day experience is perceived as having an all-embracing unity or coherence or oneness about it. And there is the resultant belief that what had previously seemed merely disparate, multiple, and unconnected is *really* a unified whole. This kind of experience — variously called panenhenic, extrovertive, the Way of Unity — is then a more specific version of that more general mode of religious apprehension in which 'the divine', 'the transcendent', 'the Real' is putatively perceived through the transfiguration of the every-day world of normal consciousness.

Secondly, we have experiences which do not involve public phenomena at all, where the world is, so to speak, 'bracketed out', and which take place 'within' the individual. There are crucial disagreements as to the nature and variety of these inner, introvertive experiences. But the accounts we will be analysing would all concur that such experiences arise as a result of following particular, more or less well-defined, contemplative or meditative paths, the parameters of which are established by and within particular religious traditions. And, without putting too fine a point on it, all would agree that, for those who have them, they give knowledge of a reality 'beyond', 'behind', or 'within' the world of public phenomena.

Let me now turn to the question of the connection between the two fronts along which this study proceeds — on the one hand, the resolution of the problem of conflicting truth claims by appeal to religious experience, and on the other, the description and classification of mystical experience. In the first half of this study, I shall take a number of major analyses of mystical experience which have, as it were, set the stage for contemporary discussions of the nature of mystical experience. This will enable us, within the context of a number of views of the nature of mystical experience and its relation to religious doctrine, to perceive the difficulties inherent in proceeding from accounts of the nature of mystical consciousness to assertions about the nature of the experiences which precipitated them. By so doing, I shall show that the proposed resolutions of the problem of conflicting religious truth claims are crucially dependent on the methodological presuppositions brought to bear on the question of describing and classifying mystical experiences. Thus, the *validity* of the appeal to mystical experience will be shown to depend on the *validity* of these methodological presuppositions.

This question of the methodological presuppositions appropriate to the classification and description of mystical experience is the particular concern of the second part of this study. I shall attempt to deal more generally with a number of possible models for the analysis of mystical experience and to develop in broad outline a conceptual framework appropriate for the empirical study of mysticism. In the light of this model, we shall then be able more readily to come to some conclusion on the validity and possibility of appealing to religious experience as a means of resolving the problem of conflicting religious truth claims.

PART ONE

Mystical Experience and its Interpretation
Some Current Theories

1

The Thesis of the Unity of all Religions:
The Theory of Sarvepalli Radhakrishnan

In order to lay the foundations for this work, we shall begin by examining Sarvepalli Radhakrishnan's thesis of the unity of all religions. This thesis is, in essence, an attempt at a resolution of the problem of religious pluralism by appeal to mystical experience. It arises, perhaps not unexpectedly, within that melding of various religions and philosophies, namely, Hinduism. And it springs, in part at least, from the attitude of tolerance for and charity towards all sets of religious beliefs especially characteristic of some forms of modern Hinduism. The passion for the truth of certain dogmas so apparent in religions of Semitic origin has never asserted itself in Hinduism. This tolerance of Hinduism for other faiths and for variations of belief which occur under its own umbrella, was noted by the first Muslim to give serious consideration to Hinduism. Al-Bīrūnī, the Muslim encyclopaedist, writing in the eleventh century A.D., remarked,

They [the Hindus] totally differ from us in religion, as we believe in nothing in which they believe, and vice versa. On the whole there is very little disputing about theological topics among themselves; at the utmost, they fight with words, but they will never stake their soul or body or their property on religious controversy. (Quoted by Zaehner 1966:4)

The above statement is a generalization about a religion, the complexity and variety of which should always make one wary of asserting anything about it *in general*. Nevertheless, in spite of the fact that, here and there, in the history of Hinduism there have been outbursts of sectarian fanaticism, it is broadly true. The mainstream of Hinduism has always felt in principle respect for and had goodwill towards a variety of religious persuasions.

Perhaps the major modern-day Hindu proponent of this attitude of charity to other forms of religious belief is Sarvepalli Radhakrishnan. His general philosophy of life is summarized in the following extract from his book *The Hindu View of Life*. He writes (1975:38),

The Hindu theory that every human being, every group and every nation has an individuality worthy of reverence is slowly gaining ground. Such a view requires that we should allow absolute freedom to every group to cultivate what is most distinctive and characteristic of it. All peculiarity is unique and incommunicable, and it will be to disregard the nature of reality to assume that what is useful to one will be useful to everyone else to the same extent. The world is wide enough to hold men whose natures are different.

It is particularly in the religious realm that man, both as an individual and as a group, must have the freedom to accept that form of religious expression which most adequately represents the nature of the ultimately real for him. Thus, Radhakrishnan writes, 'From the Ṛṣis, or seers, of the Upaniṣads down to Tagore and Gandhi, the Hindu has acknowledged that truth wears vestures of many colours and speaks in strange tongues' (1975:27).

For Radhakrishnan, there is one 'truth', but many different ways of expressing it. The doctrines, myths, creeds, and symbols of the major world religions are but different formulations of the one 'truth', different because of the differing historical circumstances which obtained when they were expressed. For this reason, the way in which the truth is expressed is not in itself of importance. The expressions of the truth are merely tools which can be used to point us to that truth which lies beyond all of them:

Behind all the varied expressions, Brahman, Yahveh [sic], Ahuramazda, Allah, there is the same intention, the same striving, the same faith. All religions spring from the sacred soil of the human mind and are quickened by the same spirit. The different systems are tentative adjustments, more or less satisfactory to spiritual reality. (Radhakrishnan 1933:19; see also, idem, 1940)

In essence therefore, for Radhakrishnan, and according to him, for the mainstream of Hinduism from the time of the Upanishads onwards, there is an underlying core of truth standing over against or lying behind the religious traditions which, perforce, only partially enshrine it.

If the claim that there is an underlying core of truth which cannot be spoken of is to be admitted for consideration, it is necessary that Radhakrishnan should supply an answer to the question, 'Whence comes this realization that there is an underlying core of truth?' In other words, having maintained that religions are only incompatible from a relative and not from an absolute perspective (in answer to our first question), how is this to be justified? For Radhakrishnan, the answer comes from religious experience. He writes (1940: 22–23),

To say that God exists means that spiritual experience is attainable; the possibility of the experience constitutes the most conclusive proof of the reality of God: God is given and is the factual content of the spiritual experience. All other proofs and descriptions of God are matters of definition and language. . . . the authority of Scripture, the traditions of the Church, or the casuistries of schoolmen who proclaim but do not prove, may not carry conviction to many of us who are the children of science and reason, but we must submit to the fact of spiritual experience which is primary and positive. We may dispute theologies, but we cannot deny facts.

In short, according to Radhakrishnan, it is religious experience, and for him this means the mystical experience, which both *guarantees* that there is an 'Ultimately Real' which lies 'beyond' the realm of sense perception, and *entails* that the ways in which this 'Ultimately Real' is expressed in the religions of the world cannot but approximate to it and act as signposts toward it.

Such, in brief, is Radhakrishnan's resolution of the problem of conflicting religious truth claims. Let us now turn to some critical remarks on it. We shall examine three problems with his account which I shall call the problems of approximation, priority, and unity.

To clarify the problem of approximation, we shall examine criticisms of the thesis of the unity of all religions offered by Philip Sherrard and Ninian Smart. In an article entitled 'The Tradition and the Traditions', Sherrard (1974) is concerned to point out the difference between the Christian conception of the Ultimate and the Hindu conception of the same (as expressed in the Hindu school of Advaita Vedānta). According to Christianity, the Ultimate is, in the main, conceived of in personal terms. He is a Father, a Judge, a Creator, etc. By contrast, the Ultimate of Hinduism, because apprehended in an impersonal mystical experience, can only be spoken of (if at all) in impersonal terms. Thus, there is a conflict between these two different ways of expressing the nature of the Ultimate. For Radhakrishnan, as we have seen, the conflict is resolved by maintaining that, in a sense, neither is to be preferred, since both are merely approximations to an underlying core of truth.

Sherrard is however not satisfied with this resolution. He maintains that, even if it is the case that all religious expressions are but approximations to an underlying core of truth, there still remains the question as to which religion most truly reflects that core in its expression. Thus, he writes, '. . . while it is one thing to say that all traditional forms ultimately express the same universal truth, it is quite another to say that they all express it to the same degree' (1974:409). Sherrard's point may be exemplified in the following way. If a follower of the Theravādin school of Buddhism asserts, 'There is no Absolute God' and a follower of Islam maintains, 'There is no God but God and Mohammed is his prophet', then on Radhakrishnan's apparent principles, both are correct. But, surely, two such incompatible statements cannot both be correct? Sherrard is therefore concerned to enquire whether there is a means by which it might be determined which religion embodies the universal truth to the highest degree.

Sherrard's conclusion is that no such means exists. He wants to argue that any attempt by a follower of any one religion to argue that his religion embodies the universal truth or underlying core of truth to the highest degree involves a begging of the question. Why? Consider a religious believer B, who is a believer in and follower of religion M. Let us suppose that B wishes to show that M embodies the universal truth to the highest degree. Then, suppose that B argues in the following way:

(i) I maintain that I have knowledge of the conditions necessary to be fulfilled by any particular religion in order for it to be considered as expressing the universal truth most fully.

(ii) M fulfils these conditions.

(iii) therefore, M expresses the universal truth most fully.

The argument expressed above is certainly a valid one. But, of course, it is the first statement by B which raises a question, namely, *how does B know* what conditions are necessary for any religion to be considered as expressing the universal truth most fully? Sherrard argues that the conditions necessary will (and can only) be derived in any instance from the knowledge that B has of his own religious tradition, namely M. That is, criteria of religious knowledge inherent in M are the conditions which must be fulfilled. Quite clearly, this may be to assume something for which there is no warrant. As Sherrard points out, '. . . the assumption that the degree of knowledge one has through a particular tradition is the highest there is, is an arbitrary assumption or an act of faith' (1974:414).

Also, it is clear that one's estimate of which religion most fully approximates to the universal core will differ according to the tradition which one accepts and believes in. Sherrard writes (ibid., p. 411),

> . . . had one obtained one's knowledge from a tradition whose basic principles do not harmonize with those of one's own tradition, one might, and probably would, have been led to quite a different assessment of what constitutes the highest knowledge and hence of what constitutes the truly universal tradition.

In essence, Sherrard's position is that the thesis of the unity of all religions demands an answer to the question of which form of religious expression most closely reflects the underlying core of truth. Sherrard maintains that this question cannot be validly answered by any believer in one particular tradition, since in formulating the answer, the ultimate validity of the criteria inherent within his own tradition is assumed and not argued for.

A similar criticism of the thesis of the unity of all religions is proffered by Ninian Smart. His criticism revolves around the parable of the blind men and the elephant. The parable tells of a number of blind men who are holding different parts of an elephant. Each blind man believes he is holding a different object from the others for each believes his description of the part is a description of the whole. So also with religions: The Christian believes he has the whole truth, likewise the Buddhist, the Muslim, etc. Yet each in fact holds only part, the whole truth being hidden from all of them. The parallels with Radhakrishnan's thesis are clear.

In a criticism of the central point of the parable, Smart writes (1968:132),

We can describe the blind men hanging on to different parts of the same elephant as doing so because we see the elephant. The parable depends on the notion that we have eyes whereas the hangers-on are blind. In short, if one is in an advantageous position regarding the truth, one can say with confidence that others only have a partial view of it.

Smart's point is, with respect to religions, who can claim to be in such a position of advantage, whose eyes do work? Again, the claim by adherents of any one tradition that they have vision appears an arbitrary one, indeed, an act of faith.

To be fair to Radhakrishnan, the claim that he is in an advantageous position is not made overtly. Nevertheless, the assumption is present, albeit in a hidden way. Hans Küng indicates that there is no doubt that Radhakrishnan does adopt a normative stance. Regarding Radhakrishnan, he states (1967:48–49, my italics):

But when he simplifies this identity [i.e. of religions] to the point of asserting that all articulate religious statements, all revelations and confessions, all authorities and rites are relative, and the *only* thing that has any ultimate validity is that inner spiritual experience of the absolute which appears in different forms in all religions and can never be adequately expressed, then he is taking up a *dogmatic* standpoint. It is only possible to make all religions equal if the underlying formless mystical experience is being taken as an absolute.

To be sure, such covert dogmatism is not restricted to Radhakrishnan. It makes its appearance in John Hick's rejection of overt dogmatism (1977a:131):

... the needed Copernican revolution in theology involves ...
[a] radical transformation in our conception of the universe of faith and the place of our own religion within it. It involves a shift from the dogma that Christianity is at the centre to the realisation that it is *God* who is at the centre, and that all the religions of mankind, including our own, serve and revolve around him.

Hick, while appearing overtly neutral, is nevertheless normatively theistic.

I do not wish to maintain, as perhaps Sherrard implies, that it is impossible to discuss the relationship between world religions without adopting a particular religious stance which is deemed as normative for other religions. This work proceeds upon the assumption of the *equal* validity of *all* traditions as possible bearers of religious truth. Nevertheless, it is perhaps apparent that Radhakrishnan's stance is a normative one, and one which places him in a greater dilemma than, for example, Hick. For, since it is the case that Radhakrishnan operates from within a particular tradition, and since this particular tradition adopts the principle that all statements about the nature of Ultimate Reality are relatively true and not absolutely true, then it is the case that the neo-Vedāntin claim that all religious doctrines, creeds, beliefs, propositions, etc. are only relatively true is itself only relatively true.

On the other hand, a proponent of the thesis of the unity of all religions could avoid being embroiled in this kind of dilemma. He could claim that since the religious experience upon which the thesis is based is an ineffable one, that the question as to which religious tradition embodies the truth to the highest degree is an absurd one, and that the above paradox evinces the absurdity of such a question. In other words, he could claim that all expressions are equally incomplete, though what would complete them, since their 'object' is by its very nature ineffable, cannot be stated. And yet, while one can sympathize with the sense of this

statement, it still leaves one curiously unsatisfied. Can such statements as 'There is a God' and 'There is no God' be treated as
equally true expressions of the same sort of religious experience?
The nature of the mystical experience may well demand it, yet
human reason demands also a resolution. We shall leave the
dilemma unresolved in the hope that we may shed light upon it
later in this study.

We shall now turn our attention to the second problem mentioned
above, the problem of the *priority of religious experience*. We
have seen that for Radhakrishnan, the claim that there is an
underlying core of truth behind the partial expressions of it is
rendered true by the facts of mystical experience. It is the mystical
experience of inner unity which, for Radhakrishnan, brings
knowledge of the Real and the True such that all empirical knowledge is seen to have a lesser status. So also, therefore, religious
knowledge claims arising from statements about what has hap-
pened in the past, or from sets of sacred writings, or from man's
use of his reason, are discounted by Radhakrishnan. Or, perhaps
it can be said that they are given a secondary importance as those
means by which the underlying core of truth has been and is given
expression within different human circumstances. The question we
shall now examine is this: Do all religions place the same value
upon religious experience as the neo-Vedāntin philosophy of
Radhakrishnan? If religions do not place a high priority on
religious experience, then this study will be vitiated from the out-
set for it too will then be proceeding from a somewhat normative
stance.

Radhakrishnan argues that there are two distinct types of
religion (1940:21):

The religions of the world can be distinguished into those which emphasize the
object and those which insist on experience. For the first class, religion is an
attitude of faith and conduct directed to a power without. For the second it is
an experience to which the individual attaches supreme value.

Among those religions in which experience predominates, 'belief
and conduct, rites and ceremonies, authorities and dogma, are

assigned a place subordinate to the art of conscious self-discovery and contact with the divine' (ibid.).

Buddhism, Hinduism, Jainism (at least) may be counted among the religions of experience, while Judaism, Christianity, and Islam may be counted among the religions of the object. While we ought to be wary again of such a generalization (for 'experiencers' may be found in Christianity as may 'devotees of the object' be found in Eastern traditions), nevertheless, Radhakrishnan wishes to argue that religions of the object are always open to the possibility of being outmoded. This is because they confound 'eternal truth with temporal facts, metaphysics with history' (1940:21). Radhakrishnan believes that because their religious expressions are dependent upon certain events which are believed to have taken place in the past, the validity of such expressions, or the beliefs based thereupon, are affected by the advance of the historical and natural sciences.

That Judaism, Christianity, and Islam have an intimate relationship to certain historical events cannot be gainsaid. The delivery of the Torah and the Qur'ān, and the Incarnation of Christ are obvious examples. But it is the nature of this relationship, in particular its ultimacy, which is of most import. To illustrate my point here, I shall briefly advert to some aspects of Søren Kierkegaard's analysis of the nature of religious belief.

In his *Philosophical Fragments*, Kierkegaard (1936) undertakes to compare the Socratic religious mode (Religion A) with the religious mode of Jesus (Religion B). For Religion A, truth is not something external to the individual but is eternally within the individual. Thus, the Socratic method of midwifery, according to Kierkegaard, consists in the teacher bringing to consciousness that which the student already knows potentially. For this reason, the eternal truth within, brought to consciousness by the process of midwifery, has no *necessary* connection with that temporal point in which it is brought to consciousness, but only an *accidental* one. Thus, also, the teacher himself neither imparts the truth nor himself forms part of it. In Kierkegaard's words (1936:13),

From the standpoint of the Socratic thought every point of departure in time
is *eo ipso* accidental, an occasion, a vanishing moment. The teacher himself is
no more than this; and if he offers himself and his instruction on any other basis,
he does not give but takes away, and is not even the other's friend, much less
his teacher.

In Radhakrishnan's terms, for the Socratic mode, eternal truth
has no intimate connection with temporal facts, nor metaphysics
with history. For Socrates, as for the religions of experience, truth
is discovered by means of an act of conscious 'self'-discovery.

By contrast, in Religion B, the historical moment has a decisive
significance. For the teacher himself gives and forms part of the
truth, which, if it be the truth, entails, according to Kierkegaard,
that the learner is in a state of untruth. And therefore, if the
learner is in a state of untruth, then the condition for understanding the truth must be brought by the teacher. Kierkegaard continues (1936:18),

But one who gives the learner not only the Truth, but also the condition for
understanding it, is more than teacher. All instruction depends upon the presence, in the last analysis of the requisite condition; if this is lacking, no teacher
can do anything. For otherwise he would find it necessary not only to transform
the learner, but to recreate him before beginning to teach him. But this is something that no human being can do; if it is to be done, it must be done by the
God himself.

Thus, that historical moment, in which the learner by receiving
the Truth from the teacher who is the Saviour thereby realizes he
is in untruth, is of crucial import. To this extent therefore,
Christianity, for Kierkegaard, has an intimate connection to temporal facts and historical process. But, does this imply that
religions of the object are open to the possibility of being outmoded because of this connection? The answer for Kierkegaard
to this question is no, and for at least two reasons.

The first of these turns upon the nature of the relationship
between the Saviour and his contemporaries. For the latter, the
historical circumstances pertaining to the life of the Saviour are
of no import. For the historical circumstances merely provide the

moment for the disciples' appropriation of the Eternal Truth presented within the historical context. Kierkegaard writes (1936:73–74),

But though a contemporary learner readily becomes an historical eye-witness, the difficulty is that the knowledge of some historical circumstance, or indeed a knowledge of all the circumstances with the reliability of an eye-witness, does not make such an eye-witness a disciple. . . . We see at once that the historical in the more concrete sense is a matter of indifference; we may suppose a degree of ignorance with respect to it, and permit this ignorance as if to annihilate one detail after the other, historically annihilating the historical; if only the moment remains, as point of departure for the Eternal, the Paradox will be there.

The second reason arises from this. For, since contemporaneity with the historical facts is not in itself a *desideratum*, then all generations are in a like relationship to those of the first generation of believers, and therefore for these also the historical facts are only of importance in so far as they frame the Moment in which the individual may appropriate the Truth through encounter with the Eternal. Thus,

If the contemporary generation had left nothing behind them but these words: 'We have believed that in such and such a year the God appeared among us in the humble figure of a servant, that he lived and taught in our community, and finally died,' it would be more than enough. The contemporary generation would have done all that was necessary; for this little advertisement, this *nota bene* on a page of universal history, would be sufficient to afford an occasion for a successor, and the most voluminous account in all eternity can do nothing more. (Kierkegaard 1936:130–131)

This brief Kierkegaardian excursus leads me to two conclusions. Firstly that Radhakrishnan's claim that the religions of the object are *necessarily* in danger of being outmoded by the advance of the historical and natural sciences is a false one, since for Kierkegaard at least the historical moment, although necessary, nevertheless merely provides the context for the Moment of encounter with the Eternal. And secondly, and for our purposes more significantly, it is the actual encounter of man with the 'sacred' or the 'revealer' (whether such encounter be mediated through a God-man as in Christianity, or through the Torah and the Qur'ān as in Judaism and Islam respectively) which is the basis of an 'eternal consciousness'. In other words, religious experience is at the roots of both Radhakrishnan's religions of experience and his religions of the object, and this fact is crucial to our discussion.

This is not to assert that the religious experience mediated within the historical context is *of the same sort* as that to which Radhakrishnan is referring. For there is as we shall see later a marked difference between the inner mystical experience of oneness which occurs as the result of techniques of meditation and so on, and the sudden and unexpected intervention of the divine in the sphere of history. And there are within those experiences which arise as the result of contemplative practices much variation in content. But this is to move to the next problem with Radhakrishnan's account — the problem of the unity of religious experience, and the concerns of the next several chapters.

2

The Varieties of Mystical Experience: The Theory of R.C. Zaehner

In the last chapter, it was suggested that Radhakrishnan's thesis of the unity of all religions depended upon there being only one kind of religious experience, and that, the mystical experience of undifferentiated unity. In this chapter, we shall examine the claim of the late Professor R. C. Zaehner that there are varieties of mystical experience. But before doing so, it is necessary to preface the discussion with a short apologetic note.

This is to the effect that, although I have outlined very briefly the sorts of experiences which may qualify as mystical ones, it is nonetheless only possible to begin with a somewhat shadowy outline of the phenomenological contents of such experiences. This is, in part, due to the fact that definitions of mystical experience are usually of a functionalist sort and are often determined by a particular religious stance. To take but two examples, the first from Radhakrishnan, the second from Evelyn Underhill. Of the mystical experience, Radhakrishnan for example says (1940:24, my italics),

This is the fulfilment of man's life, where every aspect of his being is raised to its highest point, where all the senses gather, the whole mind leaps forward and realizes in one quivering instant such things as *cannot be easily expressed*. . . . This state of being or awareness to which man could attain is the meaning of human life. . . . God is not an intellectual idea or a moral principle, but the deepest consciousness from whom ideas and rules derive. He is not a logical construction but the *perceived reality present in each of us* and giving to each of us the reality we possess. We are saved not by creeds but by gnosis, *jnāna* or spiritual wisdom. . . . *True knowledge* is awareness, a *perception of the identity with the supreme*, a clear-sighted intuition.

It is true that, on the one hand, some aspects of the mystical experience as outlined in this passage — its ineffability, its noeticity — do correspond to some of the characteristics of mystical experience given by William James (1961:299–300), for example. However, on the other hand, the penultimate and final italicized passages quite clearly adopt as the appropriate mode for expression of such experience phrases whose provenance is the Advaita Vedāntic exposition of the Upanishads. That 'True knowledge' is 'a perception of the identity with the supreme' would not be seen either by Theravāda Buddhism, by Sānkhya-Yoga, by Jainism, or by most forms of Christian mysticism as the definitive mode of expressing 'True knowledge'. By the same token, the following passage by Evelyn Underhill which details the goal of the mystic endeavour could not be accepted as it stands by Theravāda Buddhism, Sānkhya-Yoga, Jainism, nor, I think, by Advaita Vedānta. Underhill writes, 'since the aim of every mystic is *union with God*, it is obvious that the vital question in his philosophy must be the place which this God, the Absolute of his quest, occupies in the scheme' (Underhill 1930:96, my italics).

The second reason, therefore, for beginning with a shadowy outline of the possible contents of the mystical experience is implicit within the above passages. For already it can be seen that mystical experiences, or rather definitions of them, imply philosophical systems, Advaita Vedānta in the one case, theistic Christianity in the other. And it is a major part of our task to analyse the mystical experience without begging the question in this way. For the moment, it is best to leave the question of the nature of mystical experience unresolved in the hope that in the analysis to come, something of its nature will shine through. Thus, with these apologies noted, we may now turn to the theory of R. C. Zaehner.

In a number of writings, Professor Zaehner has maintained that there are three unique and distinct types of mystical experience. These three different types of mystical experience are included within a definition of mystical experience proposed in his book *Mysticism, Sacred and Profane*. Subsequent to an exclusion from consideration as mystical of such phenomena as clairvoyance, extra-sensory perception, thought-reading, levitation, etc.,

Zaehner says that mystical experiences are those '. . . in which sense perception and discursive thought are transcended in an immediate apperception of a unity or union which is apprehended as lying beyond and transcending the multiplicity of the world as we know it' (1961:198–199).

In explication of this general definition, Zaehner is concerned to argue that there are varieties of such experience and is thereby determined to show that the assumption that mysticism is an *un-varying* phenomenon observable in all times and places (an interesting example of this assumption from a theistic perspective may be found in Arberry 1950:11) is a false one. Further to this, Zaehner also wishes to demonstrate that the thesis of the unity of all religions which is based upon this assumption ought also to be rejected. According to Zaehner (1961:198), this thesis is accepted by

. . . those generous but loose-minded persons who would have us believe that all religions are equally true . . . and that the Spirit of God manifests itself in different guises throughout the length and breadth of this wide world, adapting itself to the different conditions of men and exhibiting the One Truth here in Jesus Christ, there in Krishna or in the Buddha, or again in Lao Tzu or Muhammad.

While admitting that such a view may arise from greatness of heart, Zaehner nevertheless also wants to say that it has '. . . too often sprung from intellectual laziness which would content itself with comfortable half-truths rather than come to grips with the hard facts which so persistently and unkindly break into the fine-spun web of good intentions' (ibid., p. 198).

In the light of our discussion above and our emphasizing of the normative philosophical framework of the thesis of the unity of all religions, Zaehner's claim that such a thesis arises from either intellectual generosity or intellectual laziness is perhaps a little harsh, especially with respect to Radhakrishnan.[1] Nevertheless, whatever be the psychological facts behind the thesis of the unity of all religions, the validity of the thesis is independent of these. It is, however, dependent on Zaehner's substantiation of his claim that there *are* varieties of mystical experience, namely, panenhenic, monistic, and theistic mystical experience. We may begin by considering Zaehner's category of panenhenic or natural mystical experience.

The panenhenic experience[2] may be described as an experience of the 'oneness' of all things. It is that experience which leads to the 'knowledge' that behind the multiplicity and diversity of all finite things there is an all-embracing unity. Furthermore, the recipient of such experience has an awareness that such experience has put him in contact with the world as it *really* is. As Zaehner points out (1961:50, my italics),

In all cases the person who has the experience seems to be convinced that what he experiences, so far from being illusory, is on the contrary something *far more real* than what he experiences normally through his five senses or what he thinks with his finite mind. It is, at its highest, a *transcending of time and space* in which an infinite mode of existence is actually experienced.

This 'transcending of time and space' which for Zaehner is the essence of the panenhenic experience may be illuminated by a number of examples. Our first example comes from a novel by Forrest Reid entitled *Following Darkness* (1902:42):

And then a curious experience befell me. It was as if everything that had seemed to be external and around me were suddenly within me. The whole world seemed to be within me. It was within me that the trees waved their green branches, it was within me that the skylark was singing, it was within me that the hot sun shone and that the shade was cool. . . . I could have sobbed with joy. (Quoted by Zaehner 1961:40–41)

This passage exemplifies the transcending of space in that the self is imaged as expanding and thereby taking *into itself* the whole cosmic process. The following passage from Karl Joel however has a different perspective upon such a transcending. In this case, the self does not so much expand so as to 'imbibe' the world but rather, the normal consciousness of 'self-over-against-the-world' is abrogated. In other words, the subject-object polarity of normal waking consciousness is dissolved. Joel writes,

I lay on the seashore, the shining waters glittering in my dreamy eyes; at a great distance fluttered the soft breeze; throbbing, shimmering, stirring, lulling to sleep comes the wave beat to the shore — or to the ear? I know not. *Distance and nearness become blurred into one; without and within glide into each other.* Nearer and nearer, dearer and more homelike sounds the beating of the waves; now like a thundering pulse in my head it strikes, and now it beats over my soul, devours it, embraces it, while it itself at the same time floats out like the blue waste of waters. Yes, without and within are one. Glistening and foaming, flowing and fanning and roaring, the entire symphony of the stimuli experienced sounds in one tone, *all thought becomes one thought*, which becomes one with feeling; *the world exhales in the soul and the soul dissolves in the world.* (Quoted in Zaehner 1961:38; originally quoted by Jung 1919:198–199, my italics)

'The transcending of time' is illustrated for Zaehner (1961:36–37; originally quoted in James, 1961:384, my italics) by a letter of Alfred Tennyson. He had written,

I have never had any revelations through anaesthetics, but a kind of waking trance . . . I have frequently had . . . This has come upon me through repeating my own name to myself silently, till all at once, as it were out of the intensity of the consciousness of individuality, *individuality itself seemed to dissolve and fade away into boundless being*, and this not a confused state but the clearest, *the surest of the surest, utterly beyond words* — where death was an almost laughable impossibility.

Here we see not only the transcending of time ('death was an almost laughable impossibility'), but also the collapse of subject-object polarity ('individuality itself seemed to dissolve'), the conviction of the 'realness' of the attained state ('the surest of the surest'), and the characteristic ineffability ('utterly beyond words') of such an experience. But, while the meaninglessness of death (which I take to be the intention of Tennyson's words), gives us some clue as to the nature of 'the transcending of time', the following passage from Richard Jefferies's spiritual autobiography gives us a much clearer indication of what is meant (Happold 1970:390). For here, past and future are dissolved in the present 'now', and the dissolution of the past and the future into a series of continuous 'presents' renders the latter eternal:

I cannot understand time [he writes]. It is eternity now. I am in the midst of it. . . . Nothing has to come; it is now. Now is eternity; now is the immortal life. . . . To the soul there is no past and no future; all is and will ever be in now. For artificial purposes time is mutually agreed on, but there is really no such thing.

The passages we have been examining come from a poet, a philosopher, and several novelists. But, how does the panenhenic experience relate to mystical traditions in world religions? According to Zaehner, panenhenic experience is clearly indicated by a number of passages within the Upanishads. Consider the following passage from the *Chāndogya* Upanishad (3.14; quoted by Zaehner 1961:137):

He who consists of mind, whose body is breath (spirit or life), whose form is light, whose idea is the real, whose self *(ātman)* is space, through whom are all works, all desires, all scents, all tastes, who encompasses all this (i.e. the whole Universe), who does not speak and has no care — He is my self within the heart, smaller than a grain of rice or a barley corn, or a mustard-seed, or a grain of millet, or the kernel of a grain of millet; this is my self within my heart, greater than the earth, greater than the atmosphere, greater than the sky, greater than these worlds. . . . This my self within the heart is that Brahman. When I depart from hence, I shall merge into it.

Such a passage is certainly a far cry from our earlier examples of panenhenic expression, and this for a number of reasons. Firstly, unlike the earlier passages, there is no indication within the passage that the contents thereof are *intended as* a description of mystical experience. That is to say, this passage is neither overtly descriptive of mystical experience nor is it overtly autobiographical as our previous passages were. The relationship between this passage and any underlying mystical experience is a far more tenuous one than the relationship between, for example, the experience of Karl Joel and his description of it. Secondly, unlike our earlier passages, this passage is a highly ramified one for contained within it are the crucial Upanishadic concepts, *Brahman* and *Ātman*. To be sure, Zaehner does admit that this passage contains more than the mere identification of microcosm and macrocosm, namely 'a tentative definition of the Godhead and its relation to the individual' (1961:137). But this admission in itself should warn us against taking this passage as an expression of mystical experience to be considered on a par with those of Jefferies, Tennyson, Joel, etc.

The following passage is perhaps a little clearer; again from the *Chāndogya* Upanishad (8.1.1–3, in Zaehner 1970:200–201):

In this city of Brahman there is a dwelling-place, a tiny lotus-flower; within that there is a tiny space. . . . As wide as this space (around us), so wide is this space within the heart. In it both sky and earth are concentrated, both fire and wind, both sun and moon, lightning and the stars, what a man possesses here on earth and what he does not possess: everything is concentrated in this (tiny space within the heart).

According to Zaehner, this particular Upanishadic passage exemplifies the 'transcending of space'.[3] While this passage does evince an expansion of the self comparable with the earlier passage from Forrest Reid, there is one crucial difference. This is that the section of *Following Darkness* is quite explicitly offered as an autobiographical account of a particular experience. That is, a relationship between this passage and the experience it is expressive of may be quite justifiably posited. That relationship is by no means clear in the passage from the *Chāndogya* Upanishad, for there is no mention there that the description of the identification of microcosm and macrocosm has any direct relationship to a particular experience (though this is not to deny an ultimate dependence of such passages on an experiential datum). The point is an important one and will need fuller development later. The following adumbration will for the moment suffice. The principle which arises from the above distinction is that when an attempt is made to relate a particular text to a particular sort of mystical experience, then closer attention should be paid to *that* text in which there is an explicit relationship indicated between that text and any praeternatural experience upon which it is putatively based. With regard to the passage from the *Chāndogya* Upanishad, for example, it could be argued that this microcosm-macrocosm identification has arisen from the penchant of the earlier Vedic texts for the making of numerous cosmic identifications for the greater efficacy of the Vedic sacrificial rites, and not from panenhenic experience. Certainly, it is the case that where no explicit experiential reference is made, greater caution in exegesis is necessary.

The lack of a stated connection between text and experience is even more clear in the passage which Zaehner offers as an exemplary text for the 'transcending of time'. According to Zaehner (1970:201), the classic formulation of this aspect of panenhenic experience is *Bhagavad-Gītā* 2:12–21:

Never was there a time when I was not, nor you, nor yet these princes, nor will there be a time when we shall cease to be — all of us hereafter. . . . Of what is not there is no becoming; of what is there is no ceasing to be: for the boundary-line between these two is seen by men who see things as they really are. . . . Finite, they say, are these (our) bodies (indwelt) by an eternal embodied (self) — (for this self) is indestructible, incommensurable. . . . Never is it born nor dies; never did it come to be nor will it ever come to be again: unborn, eternal, everlasting is this (self) — primeval. It is not slain when the body is slain. If a man knows it as indestructible, eternal, unborn, never to pass away, how and whom can he cause to be slain or slay?

Neither in terms of the context of this passage[4] nor in terms of its content[5] can it be clearly seen as an expression of the panenhenic experience, certainly not to the same extent as the aforementioned section from Richard Jefferies may be seen to be such.

In summary therefore, while there is a clear relationship between the 'secular' texts and the experiences upon which these are based, there is by no means such a clear relationship between the 'religious' texts quoted by Zaehner and the panenhenic experiences upon which these are supposedly based. For this reason, the argument that the panenhenic experience is described in such 'religious' texts ought, for the moment, to be treated as unproven.

With this caveat entered with respect to panenhenic experience, we may now turn to Zaehner's category of monistic mystical experience. We shall begin by quoting a text (the *Māndūkya* Upanishad, 7) which Zaehner says is an expression of the monistic experience (1974:263; see also Zaehner 1961:153–154):

Conscious of neither within nor without, nor of both together, not a mass of wisdom, neither wise nor unwise, unseen, one with whom there is no commerce, impalpable, devoid of distinguishing mark, unthinkable, indescribable, its essence the firm conviction of the oneness of itself, bringing all development to an end, tranquil and mild, devoid of duality, such do they deem this fourth to be. That is the self: that is what should be known.

This passage, taken from the *Māndūkya* Upanishad, details the fourth and highest state of consciousness, namely the blissful state of *turīya*, which transcends the states of waking, dream-sleep and dreamless sleep. Although neo-Vedāntin doctrinal ramifications enter into Radhakrishnan's analysis of this passage, his description points quite clearly to the nature of this *turīya* state (1953:698):

Though objective consciousness [states pertaining to waking and dream sleep] is absent in both the *prajna* [state pertaining to dreamless sleep] and *turīya* consciousness, the seed of it is present in the state of deep sleep while it is absent in the transcendent consciousness. Empirical consciousness is present though in an unmanifested condition in the state of deep sleep while the transcendent state is the non-empirical beyond the three states and free from their interruptions and alterations. It is present, even when we are immersed in the activities of the waking world or lost in the unconsciousness of sleep. Man's highest good consists in entering into this, the self, making it the centre of one's life, instead of dwelling on the surface.

Radhakrishnan points here to a crucial difference between panenhenic expressions and expressions of monistic experience, a difference with which Zaehner's analysis concurs. In the panenhenic experience, in the terms described by Joel, Jefferies, Tennyson, etc., there is an involvement with the world external to the self. That is to say, the panenhenic experience is a special kind of 'sensory' experience, or, in Radhakrishnan's terms, the 'objective consciousness' is still involved. By contrast, in the monistic experience as expressed by the *Māndūkya* Upanishad and interpreted by Radhakrishnan, there is a withdrawal of senses from their objects — the experience is 'non-sensory' — and a bracketing out of conceptual content. Thus, the monistic experience means, in practice, 'the isolation of the soul [the pure self within, free from "interruptions and alterations"] from all that is other than itself' (Zaehner 1961:165). Whereas, in the panenhenic experience, the soul may be said to expand such that the whole world is within itself, in the monistic experience, the soul realizes its eternal separateness from everything which is other than itself. Zaehner writes (ibid., pp. 144–145),

. . . the sense that the individual is at one with all Nature, that all is one and one is all, does not mean that all is God and God is all. It is the realization of the oneness of Nature. It is quite distinct, and necessarily so, from any state, the achievement of which is dependent on the withdrawal of the senses from their objects; and this is the classic technique of the Hindus. For how can a sensation, the essence of which is to feel that one actually *is* the outside world, be identical with the result of a technique which uncompromisingly separates the immortal soul from all sensible images?

While both the panenhenic and monistic experiences involve abrogation of subject-object polarity and are thus unitary experiences, the former includes the 'world' whereas the latter excludes it.

Granting the nature of monistic mystical experience, Zaehner questions whether it may have different kinds of expressions. He asks, 'Does it necessarily mean the absolute oneness of the Absolute or does it not rather mean the basic oneness of each human soul as it exists in eternity?' (Zaehner 1974:263)

If the monistic experience is expressed in terms of the absolute oneness of the Absolute with the consequence that all multiplicity is illusory, then the Indian system of Advaita Vedānta is the resulting philosophy. If it is expressed in terms of the oneness of each human soul existing in eternity, then the Indian system of Sānkhya is the consequent philosophy. In order to give some flesh to Zaehner's point, I shall briefly outline the relevant aspects of these systems.

For the system of Sānkhya, matter and spirit are totally distinct since there is no connection between nature *(prakriti)* and soul *(purusha)*. Souls exist in infinite number. Each soul is a separate entity and as such is completely separate from all other souls. With the evolution of nature which ontologically comes about because of an imbalance in the three 'qualities' *(gunas)* which constitute it, and teleologically comes about for the ultimate liberation of *purushas*, the souls are drawn into nature and are imprisoned therein through primordial ignorance of their true being. Release *(kaivalya)* for the Sānkhya system is attained in the realization that the pure self *(purusha)* is not essentially part of nature but qualitatively different from it. From Zaehner's perspective, such realization comes *via* monistic mystical experience. While Sānkhya has traditionally been silent regarding the method by which such experience might be gained, its sister system Yoga is centred upon the ways and means whereby such realization might be gained. (For a succinct analysis of the Sānkhya system, see Hiriyanna 1932, ch. 11.)

In comparison to the Sānkhya system, the following passage from the founder of Advaita Vedānta, Gaudapāda, may be noted:

The divine Self conceives of himself by himself through his own magic power *(māyā)*; he alone is aware of differences. This is the certainty of the Vedānta. With his mind turned outward he modifies different states already existing in his consciousness which themselves are finite. So does the Lord mould (or imagine) the world. Those things which are inside and whose time is (measured by) thought and those things which are outside and are subject to past and future time are all simply imagined (or moulded). There is no other cause for differentiation. What is unmanifest inside and what is revealed outside is all simply imagination. ... As dream and mirage and castles in the air are seen, so is the whole universe seen by those who are learned in the Vedānta. There is neither dissolution nor origination, neither bound nor Sādhu (one who has achieved liberation), there is none who seeks release and none who is released: this is the absolute truth. ... The manifold universe does not exist as a form of reality, nor does it exist of itself. It is neither separate nor not separate (from

Brahman): this is known by those who know the truth. . . . Thus knowing the Self to be such, one should fix one's mind on the non-dual. (*Kārikā*, 2, quoted by Zaehner 1961:154–155)

Whereas for Sānkhya, release comes about through the realization of the ontological difference between matter *(prakriti)* and spirit *(purusha)*, in Advaita Vedānta, liberation is attained through the realization of the One, and the consequent illusoriness of the many. Further, the 'eternal' does not consist of a multiplicity of liberated souls, but rather there is only the 'one' Reality — Brahman. That which the Sānkhya accepts as ontologically real *(prakriti)*, Advaita Vedānta denies as ontologically ultimate denoting it as *māyā*.[6]

With the main outlines of panenhenic and monistic experience as expounded by Zaehner etched in, let me turn to a question of inconsistency in his analysis, not to cast stones at Zaehner for the sake of it (for in the area of philosophy and mysticism one cannot be 'without sin' oneself), but rather in the hope that in the recognition of a problem, a resolution may at some point be arrived at.

We have noticed already that sharp lines are drawn by Zaehner between panenhenic experience and monistic experience, at least in so far as we have remained particularly within the ambit of *Mysticism, Sacred and Profane*. In *Concordant Discord*, to which we have already referred while examining panenhenic experience, the analysis is significantly different. As mentioned earlier (see note 3), the category of panenhenic experience is divided into the components of 'transcendence of space' and 'transcendence of time'. But further, the monistic experience is now seen as emerging from the *convergence* of 'the transcendence of space' and 'the transcendence of time' (Zaehner 1970:202). In other words, the monistic experience is seen as a development of the panenhenic experience. Sānkhya and Advaita Vedānta are now viewed as two possible interpretations of the monistic experience converging from the panenhenic.

A number of points are worthy of mention. Firstly, the variant analyses give some credence to my aforementioned concern over

the relationship between mystical texts and panenhenic experience. For, quite clearly, Zaehner himself views the relationship as
a tenuous one. But further, and this is perhaps of more importance, the boundaries between panenhenic mystical experience and
the monistic variety may be more fluid than Zaehner overtly
admits. But they *are* succinctly reflected in his subtly changing
analysis over a period of time.[7] We shall need to investigate this
relationship much more closely in pages to come. Our third point
relates to this. Since Advaita Vedānta includes a theory of the
cosmos within its ultimate perspective (that is, that it is *māyā*) and
for this reason appears to have possibly some relation to
panenhenic modes of expression, and since Sānkhya with its radical rejection of this *prakritic* realm thereby includes no cosmology in its view of the nature of the ultimate state (that is, an
infinity of souls in isolation from *prakriti*), the question as to
whether both of these systems may justifiably be taken as *merely*
variant expressions of the *one* kind of experience needs to be fore-
shadowed for future development.

For Zaehner, the major criterion for distinguishing between monistic and theistic mystical experience is that, while both are experiences 'within' the self, theistic mysticism maintains the distinction
between man and God whereas monistic mysticism obliterates it:

Here, then, are two distinct and mutually opposed types of mysticism — the
monist and the theistic. This is not a question of Christianity and Islam *versus*
Hinduism and Buddhism: it is an unbridgeable gulf between all those who see
God as incomparably greater than oneself, though He is, at the same time, the
root and ground of one's being, and those who maintain that soul and God are
one and the same and that all else is pure illusion. (1961:204)

From this analysis of the difference between monistic and theistic
mysticism, it is difficult to see how Sānkhya, which does not
recognize the existence of an Ultimate Being, identification with
which brings realization, can be accused of obliterating the distinction between man and God. (Again, the necessity of an answer
to the question raised at the end of the last section may be noted.)

Nevertheless, it is probably true to say, as Zaehner does, that in so far as we are speaking of Advaita Vedānta, the Vedāntin is denied that experience of the love of God which Zaehner claims is the essence of the theistic mystical experience. Thus, of the monist, Zaehner remarks (1961:168–169),

. . . so long as he sticks to his monistic view of life and feels that his philosophy is confirmed by his experience, then I do not think that his bliss can be identical with that experienced and described by the Christian and Muslim mystics (in so far as these remain theist) whose bliss consists rather in the total surrender of the whole personality to a God who is at the same time Love.

Similarly also, of monism, 'And in monism there can be no love, — there is ecstasy and trance and deep peace . . . but there cannot be the ecstasy of union nor the loss of the self in God which is the goal of Christian, Muslim, and all theistic mysticism' (ibid., p. 172).

But, not only is theistic mystical experience a different kind of mystical experience, for Zaehner it is a higher form. Indeed, he wants to maintain that, in Christian, Hindu, and Muslim mystical writings, the monistic experience may be seen to be transcended in the higher experience of the soul's union with God in love. Since this relationship will be of considerable importance in a later part of this study, it is fruitful at this juncture to detail the specific texts and then to address ourselves to the question as to whether such texts may be seen as suggesting that theistic mystical experience transcends monistic experience.

With reference to Christian mysticism, Zaehner makes much of the writings of the Flemish mystic, Jan van Ruysbroeck. In particular, it is his attacks on the Brethren of the Free Spirit (the quietists) to which Zaehner points. He quotes Ruysbroeck (1952) to this effect (Zaehner 1961:172):

. . . all those men [i.e. the quietists] are deceived whose intention it is to sink themselves in natural rest, and who do not seek God with desire nor find Him in delectable love. For the rest which they possess consists in an emptying of themselves, to which they are inclined by nature and by habit. And in this natural rest men cannot find God. But it brings man indeed into an emptiness which heathens and Jews are able to find, and all men, however evil they may be, if they live in their sins with untroubled conscience, and are able to empty themselves of all images and all action.

Zaehner argues that the experience of these quietists is an example of monistic experience. As such the emptiness and rest which is attained 'is only the purification of the vessel which can, if it will, be filled with God' and is thereby only a 'prelude to Holiness' (ibid., p. 173).

In so far as Hindu mysticism is under consideration, Zaehner points in particular to the only classical Hindu text which claims to be a direct revelation from God, namely the *Bhagavad-Gītā*. According to Zaehner (1970:205), that experience in which the sage realizes his own identity with the God-head is transcended by an experience in which the soul enters into God:

In the Gītā the mystical stages are clearly defined. First there is the integration of personality into its immortal ground which is the same in all beings, and this leads to 'liberation', that freedom of the spirit implied in the phase 'to become Brahman'. Then *after* becoming Brahman the mystic communes with Krishna in love and so finally enters into him. But both Krishna's love and the love of the mystic remain, as the last chapter of the Gītā makes abundantly clear. This means that in eternity personal relationships at least as between the soul and God remain, though transformed onto a higher plane.

Let me adopt a critical stance once again in order to illuminate a number of questions arising from Zaehner's case for theistic mysticism. Firstly, that Ruysbroeck (among others) and the *Bhagavad-Gītā* regard theistic mystical experience as the attaining of a higher state than monistic experience is not sufficient reason for claiming that it is so.[8] Within Advaita Vedānta, the opposite stance is adopted. The recognition of the separateness of God and man, and the worship and devotion which follow from this recognition, are means for the concentrating of the mind and are ultimately themselves transcended by the realization of the oneness of Brahman.[9]

Secondly, one might be willing to give credence to Ruysbroeck and to the *Bhagavad-Gītā* that theistic mystical experiences are higher than monistic if there were clear autobiographical evidence that this was the case. That is, if it could be shown convincingly that Ruysbroeck had himself claimed to go beyond a monistic state by entering into union with God or that the 'author' of the *Bhagavad-Gītā* was quite consciously outlining a contemplative path which he himself had trod, then the argument that theistic mystical experience is 'experientially' transcendent to monistic might be substantiated. Unfortunately, Ruysbroeck appears only to be criticizing the states attained by others, and the *Gītā* is clearly not a model of the contemplative path. In both cases, there would appear to be a gap between the claim that theistic mystical experience is a higher form of mysticism and the experiential data which might validate such a claim.[10] To a large extent therefore, I am reiterating in a slightly different context that principle which was announced when we examined the alleged relationship between certain mystical texts and the panenhenic experience; namely that, when it is maintained that a particular mystical experience is a higher form of mystical experience, then that claim needs to be firmly based on the actual experience of such transcending of a lower form by a specific individual.

Thus, on the face of it, and from a textual basis, there does not appear to be sufficient reason for agreeing with Zaehner's claim that theistic mysticism is a higher form, nor is it particularly easy to see why Zaehner himself argues that it is, for he himself recognizes that the Vedāntin alternative is a possible one. One possible reason is that Zaehner himself *believes* that it is a higher form. In his 'Introduction' to *Mysticism, Sacred and Profane*, he admits to stressing theistic mystical experience 'because I happen to believe that it is true' (1961:xvi). Even if it is the case that Zaehner's own beliefs have influenced his analysis (and blame should perhaps be apportioned, not for having done so, but rather for being unaware of it, for no one approaches a conceptual problem with a mental *tabula rasa*), such a criticism of Zaehner as is made by the Indologist Frits Staal should be firmly rejected. Of Zaehner's book, *Hindu and Muslim Mysticism*, he writes (1975:73–74),

... the main difficulty with this book as a whole is the author's own religious allegiance, which clearly prevents a fair and adequate description and evaluation of differing points of view and which led the author to a classification which is nothing but a reflection of his own belief.

There is of course a world of difference between Zaehner's admission that he emphasizes theistic experience because of his own beliefs and Staal's claim that he classifies mystical experience as he does to intentionally (presumably) reflect his beliefs. Therefore, rather than enter into debate on Zaehner's motives in this matter, I shall turn to a text offered by Zaehner from the Islamic context. Consideration of this text will enable us to ask the question as to whether theistic mystical experience may be considered to be a separate variety of mystical experience *at all*. Because of the importance of this question within our study as a whole, I shall quote it *in extenso*. The passage is from the *Mishkāt al-Anwār* of Abū Hāmid al-Ghazālī (quoted by Zaehner 1961:157–158):

The mystics, after their ascent to the heavens of Reality, agree that they saw nothing in existence except God the One. Some of them attained this state through discursive reasoning, others reached it by savouring it and experiencing it. From these all plurality entirely fell away. They were drowned in pure solitude: their reason was lost in it, and they became as if dazed in it. They no longer had the capacity to recollect aught but God, nor could they in any wise remember themselves. Nothing was left to them but God. They became drunk with a drunkenness in which their reason collapsed. One of them said, 'I am God (the Truth)'. Another said, 'Glory be to me! How great is my glory', while another said, 'Within my robe is naught but God'. But the words of lovers when in a state of drunkenness must be hidden away and not broadcast. However, when their drunkenness abates and the sovereignty of their reason is restored, — and reason is God's scale on earth, — they know that this was not actual identity, but that it resembled identity as when lovers say at the height of their passion:
   'I am he whom I desire and he whom I desire is I; We are two souls inhabiting one body.'
... There is a difference between saying, 'The wine *is* the wineglass', and saying, 'It is as if it were the wineglass'! Now, when this state prevails, it is called 'naughting' (*fanā*) with reference to the person who experiences it, or the 'naughting beyond naughting', for (the mystic) becomes naughted to himself and naughted to his own naughting; nor is he conscious of himself in this state,

nor is he conscious of his own unconsciousness; for were he conscious of his own unconsciousness, he would be conscious of himself. This condition is metaphorically called identity with reference to the man who is immersed in it, but in the language of truth (it is called) union. Beyond these truths there are further mysteries the penetration of which is not permissible.

The above text is an ambiguous one on a number of levels, and Zaehner's exegesis of it reflects this ambiguity. The ambiguity arises from the fact that it doesn't appear clearly to reflect monistic mystical experience in either a Sānkhyin or Vedāntin mode of interpretation. Nor does the experience itself fit in Zaehner's theistic mystical category although it's quite clear that al-Ghazālī has given the experience a theistic gloss in *his* interpretation of it. Let me expand. With respect to the experience itself, it is fairly reasonable to accept that it is that of an undifferentiated unity in which the subject-object polarity of normal consciousness is completely abrogated. As Zaehner himself admits, there are close similarities between the state described here and the state of *turīya* in the *Māndūkya* Upanishad. Yet of an experience of this sort, we have already seen that Zaehner maintains that there are two possible modes of interpretation, the one — the isolation of the individual life monad (*purusha*), the other — the realization of the absolute identity of the self and the Godhead (*Ātman* is *Brahman*). But, here, there is neither the isolation of the soul, nor the realization of the identity relation of man and the Godhead, but rather, the experience is interpreted by the mystics (al-Ghazālī apparently excepted) as the realization that the only real existent is God (in *fanā* 'Nothing was left to them but God'). As Zaehner remarks, 'the Muslim starts with the dogma that God alone is Absolute Being and that all things perish except His face' (1961:158). If this is monistic mystical experience then it is expressed quite differently from the Sānkhyin and Vedāntin versions.

But further, and perhaps more important is the gloss placed upon this experience of undifferentiated unity by al-Ghazālī. For while admitting on the one hand that phenomenologically the experience is one of undifferentiated unity and that therefore it appears as if a monistic interpretation is valid, yet he alleges on the other hand that the proper interpretation is one of union between the soul and God, and likens the seeming undifferentiatedness to the seeming unity of two lovers at the height of their passion. In other words, he appears to be thrusting onto an experience — which phenomenologically would most appropriately merit a form of monistic interpretation — an interpretation of a theistic kind and presumably for the apologetic purpose of giving certain Islamic mystical experiences an orthodox flavouring. This raises a crucial question. Since, in this case, a theistic mystical interpretation is being placed upon an experience of undifferentiated unity, should theistic mystical experiences be considered a separate category of mystical experience at all, or are theistic mystical interpretations merely a different mode of interpreting the one kind of interior mystical consciousness? With respect to the above quoted passage, I believe that an affirmative reply should be given to the latter alternative for the reasons stated. But, as one swallow maketh not a summer, neither does one example of theistic mystical interpretation of a non-theistic mystical experience (in Zaehner's sense) rule out the possibility of phenomenologically theistic mystical experience. Suffice it therefore for the moment that the question has been raised and will occupy us considerably throughout this study. By way of concluding this section it is perhaps worth noting that the possible fluidity of monistic and theistic experience and the interpretation of them is remarked upon by Zaehner himself: 'Though there is a difference, and a real difference, between the Vedāntin and Christian ways of defining the unitive experience, the difference may well be *only one of terminology*' (1961:33, my italics).[11]

Our earlier question as to which of the two varieties of interior mysticism, theistic or monistic, is higher, will of course be dissolved if it is the case that the theistic mystical experience is not a different category of mystical experience but rather that theistic mystical and monistic interpretations are merely different expressions of what is but one experience.

By way of summarizing this chapter, it is perhaps sufficient to draw attention to those critical questions which have arisen in the course of it. Firstly, what is the relationship between certain forms of mystical text and panenhenic experience? And secondly, are there varieties of interior mystical experience and can these be determined by textual analysis? These questions shall occupy us further in the next chapter.

3

The Mystical, the Numinous, and Religious Traditions: The Theory of Ninian Smart

In the Introduction to this volume, it was indicated that we would proceed from the perspective that questions of religious truth might appropriately be considered by reference to religious experience. To this extent, this study stands in a tradition which leads from such as Joachim Wach (1951) to Rudolf Otto (see Chapter 5) and thence to Friedrich Schleiermacher (1958). The basic presupposition of these three investigators of the connection between religious experience and religious expression is summed up in Wach's belief (1944:45–46) that

... if we can only pierce deeply enough through the coating of customs and ideas which are really only outward manifestations and lay bare the basic attitude conceived and nurtured by a decisive religious experience, then the various factors of religious expression will become immediately intelligible, and seemingly divergent and incongruent thoughts and acts will be found to contain one central motivation.

To begin to enter into dialogue with the writings of Wach, Otto, and Schleiermacher, one must be willing to begin from the following presuppositions: Firstly, that there is within human nature a capacity for religious experience; secondly, that religious experience is at the basis of all religion and that all religious expression is ultimately referable to it; thirdly, that this religious experience, in all its forms, reflects a single 'ultimate reality' (I am indebted to C. M. Wood (1975) at this point).

Ninian Smart also stands firmly in accordance with this tradition (see, for example, the preface to Smart 1958), in that he too quite clearly wishes to keep in the forefront of his writings the relationship between experience and expression. There is little doubt that Smart would accept the first two presuppositions above. He would not, however, be in agreement with the third presupposition, and perhaps for the following two reasons.

Firstly, if we take it as a hermeneutical principle of any investigation of religious texts that in such investigation, there is always an interplay between the meaning of the text and the 'pre-understanding' which the interpreter brings to the text in order to elicit its meaning, then Wach, Otto, and Schleiermacher bring to any religious text with which they deal the pre-understanding reflected in the third presupposition above. To this extent, the text is forced to 'fit' the presuppositions implicit in the approach to the text.[1] By contrast, for Smart the texts are allowed to stand much more (but not completely) independently of such hermeneutical devices, at least with respect to the question as to whether religious experiences are reflective of a *single* 'ultimate reality'. Thus, we find in Smart, not so much an ontological quest for the nature of such an 'ultimate reality' but rather an analysis of the phenomenological content of religious experience as such. It is the relation between forms of religious expression and the nature of the two major forms of religious experience — the numinous and the mystical[2] — as analysed by Smart with which we shall be concerned in this chapter. We shall begin with a consideration of Smart's analysis of the mystical experience.

In the course of the last chapter I argued that the relationship between certain religious texts and Zaehner's category of panenhenic experience was not as clear cut as Zaehner indicated. That panenhenic experience played a large part in religious expression was thereby opened to some critical doubt. In the writings of Ninian Smart. there is little doubt that according to Smart, the panenhenic experience plays little part in the formation of mystical expression in the mystical texts of the major world religions.

To be sure, it is difficult to perceive in any of Smart's writings a definition of mystical experience. Nevertheless, in a number of places Smart does give an indication of how he would delimit the use of the words. Thus, for example, he writes (1958:55),

Let us say that a mystical experience is one which is reported by a class of persons generally referred to as 'mystics' — such men as Eckhart, St. John of the Cross, Plotinus, the Buddha, Śaṅkara and so on. Such men are characterized by spirituality and asceticism and pursue a certain method.

While such a delineation avoids the dilemma of interpreting mystical experience from the viewpoint of a prior understanding of it, it nevertheless does rule out the possibility of the inclusion of Zaehner's panenhenic variety of mystical experience within the category of the mystical. As may be seen from our earlier examples of panenhenic experience, the experience 'of Nature in all things or of all things as being one' (Zaehner 1961:50) is, at least in the cases of Reid, Joel, and Jefferies, very much a *spontaneous* experience, one which occurs unexpectedly.[3] That is to say, the experience has not occurred as the result of the pursuit of a particular contemplative method. Moreover, since such contemplative methods occur within the confines of particular religious traditions, such men as Reid, Joel, and Jefferies could not be characterized as spirituals or ascetics in the sense that the Buddha, Eckhart, and Shankara were, since their asceticism and spirituality has meaning only within the criteria of spirituality accepted by their respective traditions. Indeed, that Smart does exclude the panenhenic experience from consideration is quite apparent when he remarks in his *The Yogi and the Devotee* (1968:66) that he wishes to reserve the term 'mystical' for those experiences which are both the result of contemplative techniques (and therefore not spontaneous), and interior (as opposed to the exterior vision of the unity of Nature). Although Smart admits that the panenhenic experience may help 'to reinforce the Absolutism of the Upanishads, Shankara and the Mahāyāna' (1968:69), there is no discussion in the Smartian corpus as to how such reinforcement takes place. In summary therefore, in so far as the panenhenic experience forms no part of Smart's conceptual framework, Smart's analysis is at variance, not only with Zaehner's, but also, as we shall see later, with the analyses of Stace and Otto. At a later point in this chapter, it will be argued that Smart's criteria for such an exclusion may well be arbitrary. For the moment however, we shall investigate Smart's critique of Zaehner's monistic and theistic categories.

While Smart does exclude Zaehner's category of panenhenic experience from his account of the relation between experience and expression, it is above all Zaehner's distinction between monistic and theistic mysticism which Smart wishes to attack. This attack is based on the claim that Zaehner has failed to distinguish sufficiently between mystical experience and its interpretation; and this for two reasons. Firstly, Smart argues that Zaehner fails to realize that different interpretations may have degrees of ramification; that is, that the interpretation of the experience may have a greater or a lesser dependence on religious concepts, doctrines, etc. which have no direct connection with such experience:

It is to be noted that ramifications may enter into the descriptions either because of the intentional nature of the experience or through reflection upon it. Thus a person brought up in a Christian environment and strenuously practising the Christian life may have a contemplative experience which he sees *as* a union with God. The whole spirit of his interior quest will affect the way he sees his experience; or, to put it another way, the whole spirit of his quest will enter into the experience. On the other hand, a person might only come to see the experience in this way after the event, as it were: upon reflection, he interprets his experience in theological categories. (1965a:79)[4]

Secondly, Smart argues that different interpretations may be made from different points of view. Thus, '. . . if a Christian says that the Buddha's Enlightenment-experience involved some kind of interior vision of God, he is describing the experience from his own point of view and not from that of the Buddha' (1965a:80). He continues (ibid.),

We crucially, then, should distinguish between a mystic's interpretation of his own experience and the interpretation which may be placed upon it from a different point of view. In other words, we must distinguish between what may be called *auto*-interpretation and *hetero*-interpretation.

In accordance with the methodological principles thus established, Smart generates the following possibilities for descriptions of mystical experience (1965a:81):
(i) Auto-interpretation with low degree of ramification;

(ii) hetero-interpretation with low degree of ramification;
(iii) auto-interpretation with high degree of ramification;
(iv) hetero-interpretation with high degree of ramification.

Smart utilizes these possibilities to criticize Zaehner in a number of ways. Firstly, Smart takes Zaehner to task for his classification of Buddhism as a form of monistic mysticism, that is, a mysticism of the isolation of the soul from all that is non-soul. Against Zaehner's assertion that the Buddha taught a doctrine of the soul,[5] Smart argues that the doctrine of non-soul (*anatta, anātman*) is attested in the earliest traditions, and that Zaehner mistranslates and misinterprets Pali texts containing the word *'atta'* (Smart 1965a:82).[6] Further, Smart maintains, even if it were the case that the Buddha taught a soul-doctrine, the non-soul doctrine of later Buddhism still remains to be explained. If a certain connection between mystical experience and *anatta* is admitted,[7] then Smart's analysis places Zaehner on the horns of a dilemma. Either, he must admit that there is a form of mysticism which is neither monistic nor theistic (for there is neither ultimate deity[8] nor ultimate personal essence in Theravāda Buddhism), thereby recognizing the inadequacy of his classification of mystical experience; or, he must show that it is possible for Buddhism to have misinterpreted mystical experience, and hence argue that it is feasible to interpret Buddhist mystical experience monistically. Smart points out that if Zaehner were to choose the latter alternative, then, in admitting that Theravāda Buddhism might be mistaken in its auto-interpretation, might it not be the case that the interpretation proffered by a Christian mystic with a high degree of ramification is also mistaken, and thus, that there is no justification for the isolation of theistic mysticism as a separate category:

If the monistic category includes heterogeneous high auto-interpretations, there is no guarantee that we should not place *all* mystics, including theists, in the same category; and explain their differences not in terms of radically different experiences, but in terms of varied auto-interpretations. The gaps within the monistic category are big enough for it not to seem implausible to count the gap between monism and theism as no wider. (Smart 1965a:83; also Smart 1968:71–72)

Thus by utilizing the principle of parsimony and a sharp distinction between experience and its interpretation, Smart maintains that all mystical experience is identical, its varied expressions occurring because of the ramifying effect of various doctrinal schemes.

Still, in spite of the Ockhamistic appeal of the Smartian thesis of the unity of all mystical experience, a caveat ought to be entered at this point. On the one hand, it is certainly the case that Smart's criticism of Zaehner is sufficient to cast some doubt upon Zaehner's classification, specifically, that Zaehner's category of monistic experience is too broad to take into account the significant varieties of religious expression which are putatively expressive of such experience. Nevertheless, on the other hand, the recognition of this fault in Zaehner's account does not *necessitate* the adoption of the Smartian thesis. For, an alternative account alluded to above could be adopted. That is, the thesis could be proposed that there are as many different types of mystical experiences as there are different expressions of it. The simplicity of the Smartian thesis would still remain persuasive; yet, on the other hand, it could plausibly be argued that the aesthetic appeal of the simpler hypothesis must needs be rejected because of the weight of textual evidence pointing to the existence of a much larger number of varieties of mystical experience.

That Zaehner does not find the Smartian proposal persuasive is perhaps evidenced by the fact that I can find no rejoinder by Zaehner to Smart in any of Zaehner's work published subsequent to Smart's discussion of it. Zaehner, of course, has his reasons for not being persuaded by Smart's thesis. Prime among these is his own *belief* that theistic mystical experience is a unique and higher form of mystical experience (see Chapter two). The question of the variety of other forms of mystical experiences is irrelevant to this claim. This leads us to a consideration of Smart's second criticism of Zaehner.

To advert to Ruysbroeck's criticism of the quietists, it will be recalled that Zaehner claimed that Ruysbroeck was criticizing the quietists' monistic experience from the viewpoint of a higher experience, namely, the theistic mystical experience. Of Ruysbroeck's conflict with the quietists, Smart remarks that Ruysbroeck's comments are compatible with the thesis of the unity of mystical experience on the grounds that Ruysbroeck is not so much criticizing the quietists on the basis of their lower-order mystical experience, but rather on the basis of their incorrect auto-interpretation — incorrect, that is, on the criteria of correctness embedded in the ordinances and teachings of the Church. Thus, Ruysbroeck's high hetero-interpretation conflicts with the quietists' high auto-interpretation, but 'the experiences for all that could belong to the same type' (Smart 1965a:85).[9]

Thirdly, Smart criticizes Zaehner for having imported into his account of mystical experience his own high hetero-interpretation of mystical experience. I shall quote a relevant passage from Zaehner, and then summarize Smart's remarks upon it. Zaehner writes (1961:193),

We have already said that when the mystic claims attributes that are necessarily divine and demonstrably not human, — such as omnipotence and omniscience, — it is fairly clear that he is not enjoying union with God, but rather some sort of natural mystical experience. Apart from this important consideration it would seem that the mystic who is genuinely inspired by the divine love, will show this to the world by the holiness of his life and by an abiding humility in face of the immense favours bestowed which he always will see to be God's doing, not his own. Only such criteria can enable us to distinguish between the genuine state of union with God and the 'natural' or rather 'praeternatural' phenomena we have been discussing.[10]

According to Smart, the theological and moral criteria of mystical experience implicit within this passage (and also within Ruysbroeck's quietist criticism) do not derive from an examination of the nature of mystical experience but rather are made on the basis of criteria external to mystical experience. Thus, the theological criterion depends on the truth of certain theological doctrines (for example, that no-one is omniscient, omnipotent but God alone). So also, the moral criterion depends upon the truth of certain theological doctrines (for example, that he who has received divine grace will evidence this in holiness and humility of life).[11] To this extent then, Zaehner has imported his own high auto-interpretation of mystical experience into his account of mystical experience.

By way of summarizing this section, we may note the following. Firstly, Smart's postulation of the thesis of the unity of mystical experience need not necessarily be adopted, but his critical scrutiny of Zaehner's categories is sufficient to cast doubt on them. Certainly, Zaehner's argument that theistic mystical experience is a higher form of mystical experience, in so far as it is based on a theological stance towards mystical experience, is invalid. This lack of cogency should not however blind us to the fact that it may be possible *by other means* to show that (1) theistic mystical experience is a separate category in some specifiable instances and that (2) theistic mystical experience is a higher form. In other words, Zaehner's basic stance, while not validated by him, may be validated by alternate procedures; the issue remains an open one.

From the perspective of the Smartian thesis that all mystical experience is phenomenologically identical, then, there is the implication that the experiences of St. John of the Cross or St. Teresa of Avila are the same as the experiences of the Buddha or Shankara. If this is the case, why is it that there are such widely varying auto-interpretations? For Radhakrishnan, as we saw in the first chapter, this is to be explained by the fact that religious expression is a crude attempt to conceptualize that which, in its essence, is unconceptualizable and can only be mystically experienced. For Zaehner, the variations are explained, in part at least, by the postulation of varieties of mystical experience. During the course of the last section, I proffered the possibility that the variety in expression was dependent upon there being as many different types of mystical experience as there are expressions of it. Now according to Smart, the variety of auto-interpretations is to be explained by the interplay between two distinct, unique, and non-reducible types of religious experience, the mystical and the numinous.

In a context in which he is speaking of the Indian religious milieu, Smart asks (1968:50) what it is that differentiates the Absolutisms of Advaita Vedānta and Mahāyāna Buddhism from the soul-pluralism of Sānkhya-Yoga and the non-theism of Theravāda Buddhism:

The secret of Absolutism [he writes] is the presence of a non-contemplative element in the religion in question. This non-contemplative element is supplied in the Upanishads by the speculative sacrificialism which threw up the concept of Brahman as the underlying reality. In Shankara it is supplied by the Upanishadic concept plus the bhakti which directed itself at the personal God Shiva. In the Mahāyāna it is supplied by the bhakti directed at the celestial Lord Buddha, as unified ultimately in the truth body. In all these cases we notice the presence of bhakti and the religion of the numinous in conjunction with the practice of contemplative dhyāna.

The religion of the numinous is based upon the numinous or theistic experience,[12] the major characteristic of which, according to Smart, is the confrontation with a being qualitatively different from any previously encountered. The experience occurs unexpectedly and not, as in the case of interior mystical experience, as the result of a quest. Both the experience of the numinous and the attitude of worship give rise to a sense of the separateness of the individual from that which lies 'beyond' the world, although this is not to deny that signs of the 'numen' may be detected 'within' the world. (The so-called 'argument from Design' is a clear instance of such detection in a highly conceptualized form.) The experience and attendant *bhakti* both signalize that there is a 'great gulf fixed between the sinful worshipper and the pure and resplendent object of worship' (Smart 1958:53). Before continuing further with Smart's analysis and in order to give some flesh to what is to follow, we shall turn to Rudolf Otto's analysis of the numinous experience upon which Smart is ultimately dependent.

As a preliminary indication of the nature of theistic experience, I shall detail three passages from three different religious traditions. From Judaism, we shall consider the vision of the God

Yahweh which Isaiah has while worshipping in the temple. Isaiah (6.1–7) is reported as saying:

(1) In the year that King Uzziah died I saw also the Lord sitting upon a throne, high and lifted up, and his train filled the temple.
(2) Above it stood the seraphims: each one had six wings; with twain he covered his face, and with twain he covered his feet, and with twain he did fly.
(3) And one cried unto another, and said, 'Holy, Holy, Holy, is the Lord of Hosts: the whole earth is full of his glory'.
(4) And the posts of the door moved at the voice of him that cried, and the house was filled with smoke.
(5) Then said I, 'Woe is me! For I am undone; because I am a man of unclean lips, and I dwell in the midst of a people of unclean lips: for mine eyes have seen the King, the Lord of Hosts'.
(6) Then flew one of the seraphims unto me, having a live coal in his hand, which he had taken with the tongs from off the altar.
(7) And he laid it upon my mouth, and said, 'Lo, this hath touched thy lips; and thine iniquity is taken away, and thy sin purged'.

From the *Bhagavad-Gītā* (ch. 11), we may consider the words of Arjuna after Krishna has manifested himself in his true form. Arjuna says,

I behold Thee . . . massed in radiance, on all sides glistening, hardly discernible . . . immeasurable. . . . All the Spirits and Divine Powers that live in heaven and earth . . . all gaze on Thee in amazement . . . as I behold Thee with yawning mouths, with wide eyes agleam, my inward soul trembles, and I find not constancy nor peace. O Vishnu . . . Thou devourest . . . all the worlds around with flaming mouths; filling the whole universe with radiance, grim glow of Thy splendours, O Vishnu! . . . In a vision I have seen what no man has seen before; I rejoice in exultation, and yet my heart trembles with fear. Have mercy upon me, Lord of Gods.

Finally, from the *Qur'ān*, we may consider a passage which presages the delivery of the *Qur'ān* (53, 4–12) to Mohammed by Allah, through the angel Gabriel. Surah 53 reads,

This is none other than a revelation revealed.
One of awesome might has taught him,
One endued with strength. Standing there
He was, away on the horizon;

Then he drew near, hovering down,
Two bow lengths away, nearer still,
And what He revealed to His servant He revealed.
The heart does not lie: he saw.
Are you disputing with him, with him who saw?

In these three passages may be seen the expressions of three *theistic* experiences. Here, there is no non-duality, no dissolution of the subject-object polarity, no expression of the unity of the self and nature, nor of the isolation of the self from the world, nor of the union of God and man in love. Rather, there is exhibited the *complete and utter separateness of God and man*. The Holy Being confronts man and stands over against him. It is he who approaches man, in the case of Isaiah, to call him to be his prophet, in the case of Arjuna, to reveal himself in his true form, in the case of Mohammed, to bring God's revelation.

The seminal delineation of this kind of experience occurs in Rudolf Otto's *The Idea of the Holy*. Otto includes this kind of theistic experience within a category of religious experience which he dubs the numinous — derived from the latin word *'numen'*. According to Otto, religions may be said to consist of both rational and non-rational elements, and these, to use his metaphor, constitute its warp and woof. But, while religions considered as socio-cultural manifestations, have to do with theoretical concepts and with moral ideas, they are not ultimately dependent on such rational notions. Rather, the essence of religion is to be found in its non-rational element and this element is constituted by the numinous experience.[13] Thus, Otto maintains that the rational and theoretical concepts of religion refer to a 'Subject' which can only be apprehended in a non-rational 'unique original feeling response' which is the real innermost core of all religions, the numinous experience.

The nature of the 'subject' (Otto uses the term 'subject' to indicate that it is the Holy Being who initiates the experience) or object of the numinous experience cannot be spoken about since it eludes conceptual analysis by definition. In Kantian terms, the *numen* cannot be spoken about as it is *in itself*, since in the attempt so to do, the non-rational is inevitably expressed in the 'rational' categories of the mind. Nevertheless, Otto wishes to use a number of words which point us towards it. Thus, Otto describes the *numen*, that which is apprehended in numinous experience, as *Mysterium, Tremendum et Fascinans*. Although Otto probably intended to convey a sense of the numinous by the use of these Latin words, to be evocative and not descriptive, we may say that in the numinous experience, man comes into contact with a mysteriousness which is both aweful and dreadful, and yet is also fascinating and compelling.

Let us begin by considering the aspect of *Tremendum*. The first element of the aspect thus indicated is its awefulness. It is important to note that such an element appears in all forms of religion, from the 'daemonic dread' which is apparent in primitive religions to the purest form of theistic religion. Otto writes (1958:17),

Though the numinous emotion in its completest development shows the world of difference from the mere 'daemonic dread', yet not even at the highest level does it belie its pedigree or kindred. Even when the worship of 'daemons' has long since reached the higher level of worship of 'gods', these gods still retain as *numina* something of the 'ghost' in the impress they make on the feelings of the worshipper, viz. the peculiar quality of the 'uncanny' and 'aweful'.[14]

In the higher religions, this quality of awefulness may become that 'feeling of personal nothingness and submergence before the awe-inspiring object directly experienced' (Otto 1958:17). Yet, also, this element of awefulness is connected with the word 'wrath' considered also as an expression which is evocative of the nature of the *numen*. Otto admits that, in the process of the rationalization of the non-rational, the wrath of God has taken on moral qualities; yet still, 'Something supra-rational throbs and gleams, palpable and visible, in the "wrath of God", prompting to a sense of "terror" that no "natural" anger can arouse' (ibid., p. 19).

The second element of the aspect of *Tremendum* is its *overpoweringness* (majestas), its 'might' and 'power'. It is especially before this overpoweringness that there is the feeling of the self as being but dust and ashes, of being nothingness. In the face of the majesty of the numinous being, there is the feeling that it *alone* is the sole reality, and that the self does not exist in comparison to it. Otto exemplifies this element by a passage from James's *The Varieties of Religious Experience* (Otto 1958:22–23):

The perfect stillness of the night was thrilled by a more solemn silence. The darkness held a presence that was all the more felt because it was not seen. I could not any more have doubted that *He* was there than that I was. Indeed, I felt myself to be, if possible, the less real of the two.

The third element in the aspect of *Tremendum* is *'Energy'* or Urgency. This feature again occurs from primitive religions right up to the highest forms of theism. It is particularly connected with the wrath of God. Otto maintains that (ibid., p. 23)

... it everywhere clothes itself in symbolical expressions — vitality, passion, emotional temper, will, force, movement, excitement, activity, impetus.

Even the love of God, says Otto, may be felt as a consuming fire.

The *numen* is further said to be *Mysterium*. The word most appropriate to signify the mental reaction to this *Mysterium* is 'stupor'. For Otto, 'stupor' 'signifies blank wonder, an astonishment that strikes us dumb, amazement absolute' (ibid., p. 26). Yet, it is not only *Mysterium* because it is beyond our comprehension, but because in our apprehension of it is revealed something which is *Wholly Other*, something the nature of which is qualitatively different from our own, and before which we therefore step back in numbed wonder. Thus, in following the line of development from 'daemonic' experience to the higher forms of expression of the numinous experience,

... this element in the numinous consciousness, the feeling of the 'wholly other', is heightened and clarified, its higher modes of manifestation come into being, which set the numinous object in contrast not only to everything wonted and familiar (i.e. in the end, to nature in general), thereby turning it into the 'supernatural', but finally to the world itself, and thereby exalt it to the 'supramundane', that which is above the whole world order. (Otto 1958:29)

If the *numen* were only terrible and dreadful, religions would only be concerned with expiation and propitiation. But, the *numen* is also *Fascinans*, the devotee is drawn towards the object of the numinous experience with longing and desire for it. Otto writes (1958:36),

But in all the manifold forms in which it is aroused in us, whether in eschatological promise of the coming of the Kingdom of God and the transcendent bliss of Paradise, or in the guise of an entry into that beatific reality that is 'above the world'; whether it come first in expectancy or pre-intimation or in a present experience . . .; in all these forms, outwardly diverse but inwardly akin, it appears as a strange and mighty propulsion towards an ideal good known only to religion and in its nature fundamentally non-rational.

As one of a number of passages which Otto quotes (ibid., p. 37) from *The Varieties of Religious Experience*, we may note the following example of the moment of fascination:

For the moment, nothing but an ineffable joy and exaltation remained. It is impossible fully to describe the experience. It was like the effect of some great orchestra, when all the separate notes have melted into one swelling harmony, that leaves the listener conscious of nothing save that his soul is being wafted upwards and almost bursting with its own emotion.

Such, in outline, is Otto's analysis of the numinous experience, within which may be placed the theistic experiences of Isaiah, Arjuna, and Mohammed. The individual is confronted by the Wholly Other, the *Mysterium*, which has a bi-polar character. On the one hand, it is an object of *Tremendum*, thereby generating boundless awe and wonder in the experiencer. On the other hand, it is an object of *Fascinans*, entrancing and captivating the individual. As compared to the undifferentiated unity of some mystical experience, or if there be theistic mystical experience, the experienced oneness of man and God, we perceive in the theistic experience of Isaiah, Arjuna, etc. the quantitative and qualitative difference between God and man (see also Smart 1964a:140),[15] a difference determined by the moment of awe and wonder, yet balanced by the simultaneous moment of longing and desire.

To return to Smart's analysis after this brief diversion upon the nature of theistic experience, we may note that, for Smart, the mystical experience is the contrary of this. As compared to the spontaneity of the theistic experience, we have noted already that the mystic consciousness occurs subsequent to a quest for that experience by means of a particular method. And further, the contemplative or mystical experience is one of undifferentiated unity, subject-object polarity being obliterated. As Smart remarks (1968:42; see also Smart 1958:41),

In the contemplative state . . . discursive thought and mental images disappear. . . . If the contemplative experience is void of images, etc., it is also void of that sense of distinction between subject and object which characterizes everyday experience.

According to Smart, religions are in part doctrinal schemes. A doctrinal scheme is a system of linked propositions which are taken to be true, belief in which is one of the criteria for determination of any individual as belonging to any religion. Further, doctrinal schemes may incorporate either one or more logical strands, the two main logical strands being the numinous and the mystical. Thus, the mystical strand consists of the mystical experience, mystical discourse, plus the appropriate religious practices — meditation, contemplation, etc. The same applies, *mutatis mutandis*, to the numinous strand (at this point, I am especially indebted to Gowen 1973). Experience, doctrines, and practice form a coherent and cohesive network. Since the numinous and mystical strands are prevalent across the major religious traditions, it is possible to classify any one doctrinal scheme under any one of the following four categories:
(1) Incorporating the mystical strand;
(2) incorporating the numinous strand;
(3) incorporating both strands with predominance given to the mystical;

(4) incorporating both strands with predominance given to the numinous.

In his book, *Reasons and Faiths*, Smart wishes to determine criteria by means of which rational decisions might be made between those sets of doctrinal schemes which have incompatible and conflicting world views. In other words, Smart is concerned with determining criteria of truth in world religions. To this end, he sets out a decision procedure for justifying doctrinal schemes which depends on their ability to satisfy four types of justification criteria — basic, organic, formal, and preferential (for a succinct account of these, see Gowen 1973:221–222). Most important is the criterion of preferential justification and it is above all with this that we shall be concerned.

The criterion of preferential justification is dependent on the notion of priority decisions. Thus,

This other element in the justification of doctrines may be called the making of *priority decisions* as between strands (and we may call the justification of one doctrinal scheme as against another by appeal to priorities a preferential justification). (Smart 1958:127)

To expand, Smart's point is that within doctrinal schemes a decision is made in favour of either the priority of the mystical strand or, alternatively, the priority of the numinous strand. Thus, a priority decision between strands will result in a doctrinal scheme of types (3) or (4) above. Quite clearly also there are limiting cases of such priority decisions. These limiting cases occur in those doctrinal schemes in which only one logical strand is operative. Thus, there will be two possible types of limiting cases, *viz.*, (1) and (2) above. Limiting cases of the first kind are e.g. Theravāda Buddhism, Jainism, and Sānkhya-Yoga (Smart 1958:29–30, also idem, 1968:23–30 and 1964a:133). Limiting cases of the second kind are Judaism, Islam (excluding Sūfism), and Evangelical Protestantism (Smart 1958:29–30; 1968:77–78).

Let us now turn to a consideration of Smart's analysis of the influence of mystical and theistic experiences, and their inter-relationship, upon doctrinal schemes. Smart points out that in those doctrinal schemes which include the concept of God (or an analogue), the mystical and numinous strands produce different kinds of cosmology and theology. Firstly, the mystical strand tends to produce a philosophical idealism. With reference to the Upanishadic doctrine of Brahman, Smart remarks (1958:105),

Now it will readily be seen that an extreme idealism dovetails well with the Brahman doctrine. For in the latter we have this picture: that beyond phenomena lies a mysterious and supremely holy Reality [numinous strand]. In the mystical picture of the world as unreal we also have the picture of Reality as lying outside phenomena. The world is, as it were, a screen, and what lies outside that screen, whether that side or this, is the truly Real. Thus the mystical doctrines of spiritual transcendence and worldly illusion assimilate the Ātman even closer to that immortal being which lies shrouded behind the shifting events of this illusory world.

By contrast, the numinous strand tends to produce a philosophical realism. In the monotheistic faiths in which God is creator of the world, the reality of the world of phenomena is asserted since, '. . . a radical denial of its reality not only constitutes a slighting of the Creator, but also helps to undermine the evidence, in the shape of traces of glory in the world and in life, upon which faith has its basis' (ibid., p. 129).

While it is certainly the case that type (2) doctrinal schemes do have a 'realistic' view of the world (for the world is the stage upon which the divine action is executed and man has a part to play in bringing the world to its *telos*), there is perhaps some room for doubt as to the intimacy of the connection between philosophical idealism and the mystical strand. Certainly, in type (3) doctrinal systems — and here Advaita Vedānta would be the paradigm — the interweaving of the two strands generates such a stance. Nevertheless, philosophical idealism is not apparent in the Vedāntin or, for that matter, in the Mahāyānan sense in either Theravāda Buddhism or Sānkhya. In both of these doctrinal schemes, the world is ontically real (Murti 1960, ch. 3), and not illusory. Thus, a certain wariness as to the assimilation of philosophical idealism and mystical experience when the latter is not ramified by a doctrine of God should be adopted. To be sure, there is a moderate idealism in Theravāda Buddhism, for the world is impermanent (*anicca*) by contrast with the permanence of *nibbāna*, but such impermanence nevertheless approximates more to the flux of Heraclitus than to the *māyā* of the Vedāntin school. As a fore-shadowing of later developments in this study, I would suggest that extreme or absolute idealism tends to have a connection with the notion of divinity beyond the world but assimilated with a turning of mystical consciousness towards reflection upon this world. (Thus, I shall argue at a later point that there is an expression in mystical texts of a panenhenic consciousness that arises from interior mystical experience.)

Secondly, with reference to theology, the numinous strand tends to provide a positive theology and the mystical strand a negative theology, the latter consisting of such expressions as 'reality', 'being', 'unity', etc. Smart argues that it is of the very essence of mystical theology to generate negative or ontological theology though such expressions should not be considered as having descriptive content but rather a valuational use. Nevertheless, even though all mystics tend to use ontological language, mystics operating within a theistic tradition may be constrained by the positive theology of that tradition. Therefore, such mystics effect a compromise:

> The numinous strand will thus remain doctrinally predominant in their way of speaking, and their goal will be described in terms of Spiritual Marriage, etc.: contact with the Divine, not deification. . . . Thus the marriage analogy serves to retain the subject-object (worshipper-divine) distinction while also portraying the raptness of the soul. (Smart 1958:144)

It follows then that, according to Smart, the language of 'Spiritual Marriage', 'Union with God', 'the Union of God and the soul in love' is the closest the theistic mystic can approximate in his description to the undifferentiated unity of the mystical state without obliterating that distinction between God and the soul necessitated by the tradition in which he is operating. Zaehner's category of theistic mystical experience, based as it is upon various modes of mystical expression is, from this perspective, rejected also, for the theistic mode of mystical expression is interpreted in terms of the interplay of numinous and mystical strands.

With this delineation of the possibilities for priority decisions, we shall now consider the question of preferential justification. Smart argues that a doctrinal scheme of type (4) is preferentially justified over those schemes under type (3). That is, only those doctrinal schemes which make a priority decision in favour of the numinous strand are preferentially justified. His argument is as follows.

The preferentially justified doctrinal scheme is that one which can harmoniously incorporate both logical strands. Type (3) doctrinal schemes deny both the gap between Creator and created, and the philosophical realism endemic to the numinous strand. Thus, in such schemes, the numinous strand is obliterated:

The Absolutistic interpretation of religion thus seems to render bhakti ultimately meaningless. And this is brought out explicitly in Advaita, with its doctrines of levels of truth. Bhakti has a provisional importance only. In the experience of 'That Art Thou' all rituals and praise die away. Given, then, the principle of equality between bhakti and dhyāna, the dialectic of religious experience seems to militate against an Absolutistic interpretation. (Smart 1968:80)

By contrast, Smart claims that type (4) doctrinal schemes incorporate the mystical strand without obliterating it. The key to this incorporation is the analogy of 'love' and 'Spiritual Marriage'. Thus (ibid., p. 82),

The image of love, of the Spiritual Marriage, is the key to the equal life of bhakti and dhyāna. . . . The two intertwine, but they do not strangle one another. Both remain meaningful moments of religious experience under the wing of the right kind of theism.

Leaving aside for the moment the question of the validity of treating bhakti and dhyāna (the theistic and mystical elements) equally, it is nevertheless difficult to see how the mystical strand is any less obliterated by its incorporation into type (4) doctrinal schemes than the numinous strand is obliterated by *its* incorporation into type (3) doctrinal schemes. That is to say, if the main characteristic of the mystical strand is subject-object distinctionlessness and the major feature of mystical theology is philosophical idealism, then these would appear to be obliterated just as much in a type (4) scheme as the gap between creator and created, and philosophical realism, are obliterated in a type (3) scheme.

Further, even if it were the case that type (4) doctrinal schemes were preferentially justified over type (3) schemes, Smart's criteria do not enable the determination of which particular type (4) doctrinal scheme is to be preferred. As Julie Gowen remarks (1973:225),

If we grant Smart, for the sake of argument, his conclusion that if there is a true doctrinal scheme it will be theistic, it follows that the true doctrinal scheme will be built around the belief in the existence of a divine being. Judaism and Christianity, both theistic doctrinal schemes, characterize the divine being significantly differently, which is to say that these two doctrinal schemes embody at least in part incompatible doctrines. Smart's criteria do not suffice to tell us which is the correct or superior interpretation of the given of numinous experience.

More importantly, it is difficult to see *how* Smart within his conceptual framework *could* determine which particular scheme is to be preferred. That this is so is due, in part, to his notion of the nature of religious truth. Of religious truth, he quite appropriately comments (1968:142),

It concerns the Transcendent, it moves in the sphere of intimate experience, it is bound up with awe and bliss, it is entangled powerfully and fruitfully in symbolism. It is scarcely plausible to expect the truths of religion to be demonstrable or for the evidences to be like those of the law court or the laboratory. ... It seems sad that when our lives are to be shaped by belief there is no absolutely authoritative way of establishing that belief.

There is, however, a more compelling reason for Smart's inability to specify which particular type (4) doctrinal scheme is to be preferred, and this reason turns on his crucial distinction between experience and interpretation.

As we have seen, Smart argues that mystical experience is phenomenologically everywhere the same, and that differences in interpretation are due to the different doctrinal schemes by means of which the descriptions of mystical experience are ramified. This means that in order to determine which interpretation is the most correct description, it is necessary to examine low auto-interpretations. That is to say, if one is seeking a phenomenological analysis of mystical experience without the overlaid interpretations derived from any extant doctrinal schemes, it is fruitful to seek a variety of low auto-interpretations, to compare and contrast them, and thus derive a series of descriptive propositions which would most closely approximate to the mystical experience. And this appears to have been the method by means of which is generated Smart's description of mystical or contemplative experience as an experience of undifferentiated unity in which the subject-object polarity of everyday experience is abrogated. However, this type of analysis could not possibly bring about a resolution of the problem of which doctrinal scheme is preferable since the purpose of the exercise is to bracket out the influences of such schemes upon the descriptions of mystical experience.

But further, Smart argues (1965a:87) that the truth of any interpretation of religious experience depends in large measure on factors external to the experience. This places Smart in a conceptual bind since he wishes to maintain *both* that if we are to find religious truth, we should look to religious experience (and this as we have seen is a conceptual presupposition of Smart's approach to the resolution of incompatibility in doctrinal schemes); *and* that the truth of any interpretation depends (in part at least) on the truth of the doctrinal scheme which ramifies the interpretation (and thus the question of religious truth becomes the question of the truth of the ramifying doctrinal scheme).

This conceptual bind could be resolved by arguing that the true doctrinal scheme is the one which most approximates to the given of religious experience. In this case, one would perhaps generate the Islamic doctrinal scheme as that which most closely approximates to theistic experience (for Allah is pre-eminently the wrathful deity, yet also the merciful and compassionate one), and the Theravādin doctrinal scheme as that most closely approximating to the mystical experience. Indeed, Smart does suggest that the non-self doctrine of Theravāda is to be preferred to the soul-pluralism of Sānkhya and Jainism on the grounds that 'non-self' is a more correct description of the phenomenological content of mystical experience. He writes therefore (1964a:139),

. . . since the experience of the yogi involves going beyond the ordinary discriminations of perceptual, imaginative and ratiocinative experience, thus attaining a certain 'voidness', looked at from the point of view of the world, it is rather hard to distinguish one mystic's content of experience from another's. The undifferentiated nature of the experience thus opens the way to the abandonment of individual souls or selves, though without the implication that therefore there is just one Self. . . . Thus the Buddhist position of, so to say, starting from a pluralistic base but going beyond it is an intelligible development from soul-pluralism.

Nevertheless, even granting the close connection of mystical experience and the doctrinal scheme of Theravāda Buddhism, since candidacy for religious truth entails the incorporation of both logical strands, Smart could not resolve the conceptual bind by this means. As he himself notes (1958:157), it could be argued

that a complicated creed does achieve a degree of comprehensiveness which the simpler ones do not. For instance, Brahmanism has the advantage that it welds together both the activities of sacrifice and those of asceticism; and the Sūfi movement transformed Islām in such a manner that it became clear that one could love Allah with two loves.

Moreover, and without putting too fine a point on it, even if it were possible to base a case for religious truth on the notion of least-wide ramification, it would still be necessary to decide what was to count as grounds for being least-widely ramified without either creating a set of phenomenological criteria which could include *all* doctrinal schemes (William James's criteria of mystical experience could be seen in such a light), or committing oneself in advance to the viewpoint of any *particular* doctrinal scheme.

Alternatively, it may be possible to resolve the conceptual bind by arguing that the truth of any particular doctrinal scheme might be excogitated without reference to the given of religious experience. For example, Smart's criteria of formal justification might be seen as such extra-experiential criteria. Two such criteria adumbrated by Smart are simplicity and concealment of the Divine Being. Thus, for example, monotheistic religions are formally justified over polytheistic religions, and non-idolatrous religions over idolatrous ones. Nevertheless, and excluding the question as to the validation of these criteria, in that we would then be faced with deciding between a number of monotheistic, non-idolatrous systems, we would be required to either expand our formal criteria, or return to the given of religious experience. Validation of the former (if such could be found) would be a necessary requisite; adoption of the latter, as we have seen, only exacerbates the problem. Thus, in conclusion, in that Smart appears committed to seeking religious truth by appeal to religious experience (both mystical and theistic) and *outside of it*, and since Smart's framework does not allow resolution of this dichotomy, the conceptual bind remains.

As we have seen throughout this chapter, crucial to Smart's analysis is the phenomenological unity of mystical experience. We have already entered a caveat with respect to the validity of this thesis, and shall now consider a further criticism of it. As noted above, the mystical experience is an interior experience, an experience 'in the depths of the soul' (Smart 1964a:131). As such, it is to be contrasted with the panenhenic experience of the unity of nature as outlined by Zaehner. Smart, in contrast to Zaehner (and also, as we shall see, to W. T. Stace and Rudolf Otto), excludes this experience from the category of mystical experience. In the second chapter of this study, some questions were raised as to the interpretation of certain texts as reflecting panenhenic experience. Our task, for the moment however, is to determine whether Smart's exclusion of panenhenic experience is justified.

Smart's criteria for the exclusion of panenhenic experience are that it neither follows from the pursuit of a contemplative method, nor is it phenomenologically compatible with the experiences of such men as are called 'mystics'. I shall attempt to show that Smart's second criterion is either circular and therefore arbitrary, or that it collapses into the first criterion. I shall then argue that the first criterion is not sufficiently justified as a necessary criterion for the application of 'mystical'.

With reference to the second criterion, it is fruitful to ask the question what it is that such men as St. John of the Cross, the Buddha, Shankara, etc. have in common which entails that their experiences are mystical ones. This question arises from the consideration that if these men are to function as paradigms of the sorts of people who have mystical experiences, it is necessary to indicate a common factor among them apart from or in addition to their being the recipients of these sorts of experiences. Smart appears to suggest, in part at least, that what they have in common is the fact that they are *called* 'mystics'. But, this is tantamount to saying that mystical experiences are had by these men because they are called 'mystics' and, in the absence of any other defining characteristic of 'mystics', they are called 'mystics' because they have mystical experiences. In other words, Smart appears to be involved in circularity at this point and his choice of these individuals as paradigmatic and the exclusion of such as Joel, Jefferies, etc. has a hint of arbitrariness about it.

Still, Smart's first criterion does attempt to show that there is a common factor among these mystics which is additional to and, to a large extent, separate from the experience itself. That is, the justifying criterion for their being the recipients of mystical experiences is that they all followed some particular ascetical path. In this way, therefore, the second criterion may be seen as dependent upon the first. Nevertheless, it is necessary to give reasons why the predication of 'mystical' to any experience is dependent on the fulfilling of this first criterion. This is of course not to deny that there is a connection between the attainment of mystical experience and the treading of a contemplative path. Such a contingent relationship is attested in all the major mystical traditions. But to argue 'no contemplative method, therefore no mystical experience' is a far stronger claim than is implied in the registering of the contingent connection. In order to verify it, one would need to ascertain firstly, that no 'interior' mystical experience arises spontaneously; and secondly, that no non-interior (e.g. panenhenic) experience arises as the result of the pursuit of a contemplative method. This is not to criticize Smart for not fulfilling a probably impossible task, but rather merely to raise some doubts as to the *necessity* of the connection of method and experience.

There are a number of conclusions which may be drawn from the above analysis. Firstly, since neither of Smart's criteria are convincing, there is no reason to exclude the panenhenic experience from the predication of 'mystical'. This is not to assert that the panenhenic experience finds expression in doctrinal schemes, for we have expressed doubts about this in the last chapter. It is, however, to maintain that the panenhenic experiences of Joel, Jefferies, etc. cannot be denied as mystical experiences on Smartian grounds.

In one sense, this is not important. Smart's definition of what is to count as contemplative or mystical experience may be a merely stipulative one. And consequently, his denial of the predication of 'mystical' to panenhenic experiences may be intended only to remove some terminological confusion. But it does have important implications for the structure of Smart's appeal to religious experience. It facilitates the possibility of the assertion of the phenomenological unity of mystical experience because a phenomenologically different experience is definitionally excluded from consideration. And thus, it enables Smart, methodologically, to ignore to all intents and purposes the possible influence of panenhenic experience on the formation of religious doctrine. However, if it is the case that some form of panenhenic consciousness is reflected in religious expression, then this will blur the sharp outlines of the account of the relationship between religious experience and doctrinal schemes offered by Smart. And it necessitates too the revision of the Smartian thesis of the phenomenological unity of mystical experience to the thesis of the unity of *interior* mystical experience.

Secondly though, we have also alluded to reasons why this thesis ought not to be accepted as validated, for while its simplicity is appealing, this factor ought not to be allowed to prejudice the issue of whether there are, for example, phenomenologically theistic mystical experiences.

In the last chapter, we saw how Zaehner had argued that Advaita Vedānta and Sānkhya were merely different expressions of the same kind of experience, *viz.* monistic experience. Certainly with regard to these two systems, their differences are far more clearly illuminated by Ninian Smart in his assigning of Sānkhya to the mystical strand, and his classification of Advaita Vedānta by means of the notion of its interweaving of the numinous and mystical strands with the latter predominant. His further claim that expressions of theistic mysticism are not to be taken as evidence of a different kind of mystical experience but are to be seen in terms of the interweaving of numinous and mystical strands with the former predominant certainly appears to be reflected in the passage from the *Mishkāt* of Al-Ghazālī we examined earlier. That, in this passage, the undifferentiated unity of mystical experience is interpreted by Ghazālī in orthodox theistic terms is important evidence for the necessity of taking the numinous strand into account. And, from the perspective of this passage, Smart's analysis is certainly more persuasive than that of Zaehner.

In the next chapter, we examine the analysis of mystical experience offered by W. T. Stace. For Stace, neither theistic mystical experience nor the theistic experience are part of his conceptual framework. Rather, mystical doctrines are related to the presence of extrovertive experiences (Zaehner's panenhenic category) and introvertive experiences (the unity of 'interior' mystical experience being a presupposition of Stace's account).

4

Extrovertive and Introvertive Mysticism: The Theory of W. T. Stace

It has been argued in the previous chapter that Smart's failure properly to consider the role of panenhenic experience is an unfortunate one. Now both W. T. Stace and Rudolf Otto include the panenhenic experience in their accounts and see it as having a decisive role in the formation of religious doctrine. Because W. T. Stace also incorporates in his account what amounts to the thesis of the phenomenological unity of interior mystical experience, it will be useful to examine his proposals first.

In his major work on mysticism, *Mysticism and Philosophy* (1961), Stace sets out, not only to delineate the central core of mystical experience by describing those characteristics which are common to all mystical experience, but also to demonstrate which interpretation of mystical experience is the true one. Thus, like Zaehner and Smart, a study in the description and classification of the mystical experience is supplemented by a philosophical task.

After an examination of Stace's account of the two varieties of mystical experience, the introvertive and the extrovertive, we shall turn to his arguments for the existence of a Universal Self, for the notion of the vacuum-plenum paradox, and for identity in difference as the essence of mystical experience. I shall endeavour to exhibit the incompatibilities and inconsistencies which arise when we contrast Stace's phenomenological analysis of mystical experience with those claims which arise from his philosophical arguments.

The pivotal point of Stace's account relies upon his elucidation of the following question (1961:43):

Is there any set of characteristics which is common to all mystical experiences, and distinguishes them from other kinds of experience, and thus constitutes their universal core?

He primarily discounts visions, voices, raptures, hyper-emotionalism, etc. as subsumable under the category of mysticism, while nevertheless admitting that such phenomena may accompany the mystical experience. Granting the validity of this exclusion, we may note that according to Stace (ibid., pp. 131–132), all mystical experiences share the following characteristics:
(i) Sense of objectivity or reality;
(ii) feeling of blessedness, peace, etc.;
(iii) awareness of the holy, sacred, or divine;
(iv) paradoxicality;
(v) ineffability.

These characteristics, however, revolve around a nucleus which is the inner core of the mystical experience. This is the experience of a unity 'which the mystic believes to be in some sense ultimate and basic to the world' (ibid., p. 132).

This unitary experience may take either of two forms, the extrovertive or the introvertive. As for Zaehner and Smart, so also for Stace, the difference between them is that 'the extrovertive experience looks outward through the senses, while the introvertive looks inward into the mind' (ibid., p. 61). In essence, extrovertive mysticism involves the apprehension of a 'One' or 'Universal Self' through a unifying vision of the external world. By contrast, introvertive mysticism involves the 'apprehension' of an undifferentiated unity of 'pure consciousness', '. . . from which all the multiplicity of sensuous or conceptual or other empirical content has been excluded, so that there remains only a void and empty unity' (1961:110).

Without continuing to belabour a point made at some length in our discussion of Zaehner, it is worth noting that the passages from Meister Eckhart and from St. Teresa of Avila, which are adduced as examples of their being the recipients of panenhenic or extrovertive experiences, are not conclusive. This is for the reason that there is lacking in the passages cited any stated connection between these expressions and the occurrence of an extrovertive experience.[1] In this sense, these passages are quite distinct from the detailed autobiographical account offered by 'N.M.', which is closely comparable to the experiences of Joel, Tennyson, Jefferies, etc. It is 'N.M.'s' autobiographical account that is the basis upon which Stace illuminates the extrovertive experience. The passage which perhaps gives the closest apparent connection of panenhenic experience to panenhenic expression is a passage which Stace finds in the writings of Evelyn Underhill. According to Evelyn Underhill (1930:255-256, quoted by Stace 1961:69), in the life of Jakob Boehme,

... there were three distinct onsets of illumination, all of the pantheistic and external type. ... About the year 1600 occurred the second illumination, initiated by a trance-like state of consciousness, the result of gazing at a polished disc. ... This experience brought with it that peculiar and lucid vision of the inner reality of the world in which, as he said, he looked into the deepest foundations of things. ... He believed that it was only a fancy, and in order to banish it from his mind he went out upon the green. But here he remarked that he gazed into the very heart of things, the very herbs and grass, and that actual nature harmonized with what he had [inwardly] seen.[2]

Of importance here is not the fact that Boehme uses panenhenic modes of expression. Rather, the panenhenic mode of expression arises from his gazing upon the world subsequent to being the recipient of an *interior* ('inwardly seen') mystical experience. In other words, the nature of interior experience 'within the self' reflects back upon the way the individual views himself, himself in the world, and himself and the world, subsequent to that experience. To paraphrase Underhill, 'actual nature harmonized' with the content of the interior experience. In essence, panenhenic modes of expression in mystical texts arise from reflection upon the world subsequent to the interior experience.

This means, therefore, that a distinction between modes of panenhenic expression needs to be made. On the one hand, there are those panenhenic expressions which are quite clearly the result of a (normally) spontaneous panenhenic experience. We may take as certain examples of this mode of panenhenic expression *only* those cases where there is an autobiographical reference to the connection of expression and panenhenic experience. On the other hand, there are panenhenic expressions which occur as a result of reflection upon the relation of self and world, and the world *in se*, subsequent to interior mystical experience.

From this we may generate a methodological principle of some importance. This is to the effect that, subject to the autobiographical proviso above, panenhenic modes of expression are dependent upon that apprehension gained *via interior mystical experience*, and therefore, spontaneous panenhenic experience need not be taken into account in analysis of the relationship between religious experience and religious expressions. At this point therefore, we may say that Smart is vindicated with respect to his exclusion of spontaneous panenhenic experience from consideration. However, he is in error to the extent that panenhenic modes of expression arising from interior experience reflecting upon the world are not taken into account in his analysis.

Before proceeding to a more detailed analysis of Stace's account, it is necessary to outline his argument for the 'trans-subjectivity' of that experience. By 'trans-subjective', Stace wishes to indicate that neither 'subjectivity' nor 'objectivity' are suitable descriptions of the mystical experience. As his criterion of objectivity, Stace adopts the notion of orderliness. By contrast, he adopts the notion of disorderliness as the criterion of subjectivity:

An experience is objective when it is orderly both in its internal and its external relations. An experience is subjective when it is disorderly either in its internal or its external relations. (1961:140)

The notion of orderliness is further specified as '. . . law, that is to say, regularity of succession, repetition of pattern, "constant conjunction" of specifiable items' (ibid.).

To be sure, Stace's definitions of subjectivity and objectivity are by no means conclusive; they are not so much argued for as merely asserted, and there are varieties of alternative definitions.[3] Nevertheless, the point of these definitions is quite clear. Since the introvertive (or interior) mystical experience is one of undifferentiated unity, Stace maintains that it cannot be objective because, 'There are no distinguishable items or events among which repeatable patterns or regular sequences could be traced' (1961:144). By the same token, since a unitary experience cannot exhibit positive infringements of natural law by virtue of its undifferentiated nature, it cannot be subjective either. Therefore, in order to delineate that sense of objectivity or reality (i.e. William James's 'noeticity') which is one of the characteristics of the mystical experience, Stace coins the term 'trans-subjective'. Such trans-subjectivity applies for Stace to both types of mystical experience. The thrust of his argument is that claims to objectivity should not be ruled out of court on the basis of criteria of objectivity and reality which operate in the every-day world of duality and multiplicity. Mystical statements, like religious statements in general, are serious candidates for religious truth.

As indicated above, Stace maintains that the unity experienced is that of the pure self (or mind) emptied of its empirical contents. He further maintains (1961:150–151) that any one self emptied of its empirical contents cannot be distinguished from any other self in an identical situation. Thus, argues Stace, we are logically forced to postulate the existence of a Universal Self (ibid., p. 203):

. . . if the undifferentiated unity is the pure unity of the individual self, then there is no *principium individuationis* on which can be based a distinction between one pure self and another. Therefore, we cannot stop at the individual ego, but are logically compelled to pass on to a *Universal Self.*

Stace further argues that since both the introvertive One and the extrovertive One are empty of content, 'there is nothing to constitute a *principium individuationis* between them', and thus there are good grounds for the mystics' identification of the two (ibid., p. 152, also ibid., p. 110). A preliminary problem may be dealt with at this point. Stace equivocates between the nature of the experience and the 'object' of the experience. That is to say, according to his analysis, it is the experience which is contentless.

In the passage immediately above, this lack of content is predicated of the 'object' of the two types of experience, namely, the extrovertive One and the introvertive One. This equivocation is *only* justified if it is the case that the transition to Universal Self is justified.

There are a number of points against Stace's argument to the Universal Self. Firstly, as we shall see later, Stace himself admits that the notion of the pure self is an *interpretation* of the unitary consciousness attained in the introvertive mystical experience. Thus, it would follow that there is no intrinsic connection between the notion of a pure self and the introvertive experience, that is, other interpretations are possible. This implies that we are not *compelled* to posit a pure self as that which is isolated from its empirical surroundings in the introvertive experience. Hence, on these premises, neither are we compelled logically to posit a Universal Self. Secondly, even if it were the case that the notion of a pure self without empirical properties were substantiated such that there was no *principium individuationis* by means of which a plurality of pure souls can be established, this does not justify the postulation of a *single* Universal Self. As Ninian Smart remarks, 'If there is no *principium individuationis*, both singular and plural would seem to be inapposite, and there is no more need to speak of a Self than of Selves' (1962:19).

Thirdly, and from an Indian perspective, the argument against a Universal Self and an argument for the plurality of souls proceeds along the following lines. If it were the case that all souls were one, that all were ultimately the Universal Self, then what happens to one soul, ought to happen to all souls. Thus, if one soul attains release by realizing its true nature, then all souls ought simultaneously to gain release. But this is manifestly not the case for some souls attain release while others continue inextricably connected to the realm of *samsāra*. Therefore, a pluralism of souls is the true situation.[4]

Now Stace wants to argue that both the introvertive and the extrovertive experiences are self-transcending, that is, both kinds of experience point towards a trans-subjective reality. Accordingly, that the mystic apprehends a Universal Self in both types of experience helps explain why the experience is a self-transcending one. That is to say, the vast majority of mystics take the experience to be a self-transcending one because the notion of a reality beyond the individual is not part of the interpretation of the experience but is part of the experience itself (Stace 1961:153).

However, Stace's analysis is not at all clear or unambiguous; for, within several mystical systems, the notion of self-transcendence may have a variety of meanings. Thus, 'self-transcendence' can mean: Transcendence of the empirical self (as in Sānkhya); transcendence of the self (as in Advaita Vedānta in the identity of the self and Brahman); transcendence in the sense of rejection of the self in an empirical and a metaphysical sense (as in Theravāda Buddhism). As we have noted earlier, according to the Sānkhya philosophy, release consists in the realization of the absolute distinction of *purusha* (soul) from everything which is *prakriti* (non-soul). The empirical self (including the mind)[5] is part of *prakriti*. Self-transcendence in Sānkhya thus consists in the isolation of the self from the empirical self consisting of *prakriti*. By contrast, in Advaita Vedānta, the selves (*jīvas*) are only many from the 'empirical' perspective. The respective individuality of each soul is due to its adjuncts such as the senses and the body. From the absolute perspective however, each *jīva* is alike the supreme reality (i.e. Brahman) (Dasgupta 1969, I, 439–443). Such a schema reflects more closely the logic of 'self-transcendence' as outlined by Stace. Despite this, Stace himself is concerned, as we shall see at a later point, to reject the monism of Advaita Vedānta as an adequate interpretation of the mystical experience. In consonance with both Sānkhya and Advaita Vedānta, Theravāda Buddhism rejects the equivalence of the *ātman* with any psycho-physical characteristics of the individual. Yet, it also rejects the notion of a substantial soul at the basis of the individual. The notion of soul (*ātman, atta*) is transcended by *nairātmya-vāda* (doctrine of no-self) (see, for example, *The Questions of King Milinda*, 2.1.1). Thus, in both Sānkhya and Theravāda Buddhism, different notions of self-transcendence can be discerned, the former rejecting the empirical self as the absolute, the latter rejecting the notions of both empirical and metaphysical selves. Further, in neither of these systems does the Universal Self have a place. In summary, this brief analysis indicates the tenuousness of the adoption of 'self-transcendence' as a means of vindicating the concept of a Universal Self.

Now according to Stace, the essence of the concept of the Universal Self is found in the concept of the vacuum-plenum paradox. He argues that there is a tension within the concept of the Universal Self between positive emphases (the *plenum*) and negative emphases (the *vacuum*). He maintains that these emphases or modes of expression are found in tension with each other in all religions and philosophies in which mysticism plays a part. On the one hand, the Universal Self has qualities; it is personal, creative, dynamic, and active (the *plenum* aspect). On the other hand, it is qualityless; it is impersonal, inactive, static, and motionless (the *vacuum* aspect). It is difficult, however, to see the connection between the Universal Self as the contentless One and the Universal Self as exhibiting the vacuum-plenum paradox, and this for a number of reasons. Firstly, it is certainly feasible to argue that the negative predications of the vacuum-plenum paradox are refusals to predicate anything of the Universal Self (the *via negativa*) and thus to show that there is a subtle interplay between the contentless (and thus ineffable) One and the desire to describe it (see Mortley 1975:377). On the other hand, however, there appears to be a *prima-facie* incompatibility between a contentless One and the predication of positive attributes. In effect, having registered the phenomenon, Stace is at a loss to explain it. It is certainly the case that the vacuum-plenum paradox is generated in the *Bhagavad-Gītā*, in the writings of Shankara, in Mahāyāna Buddhism, in Pseudo-Dionysius, in Eckhart, and in the Eastern Orthodox tradition of mystical theology.[6] Yet, it is conspicuously absent in those systems which, if we work on a Smartian model at this point, epitomize mystical religion, namely, Theravāda Buddhism, and Sānkhya, the former of which is recognized by Stace himself (1961:43) to be a test case for any theory of mysticism. Thus, with regard to Theravāda Buddhism, and by stretching a point in allowing *Nibbāna* and the Universal Self to be compared, I can find no evidence of positive predication with respect to *Nibbāna* in Johansson's (1969:112–113) semantic differential for *Nibbāna*. Indeed, to the contrary, perhaps the most famous discourse on *Nibbāna* is couched in almost totally negative terms:

There is that sphere wherein is neither earth nor water nor fire nor air; wherein is neither the sphere of infinite space nor of infinite consciousness nor of nothingness nor of neither-ideation-nor-non-ideation; where there is neither this world nor a world beyond nor both together nor moon and sun; this I say is free from coming and going, from duration and decay; there is no beginning and no establishment, no result and no cause; this indeed is the end of suffering. . . .

Monks, there is a not-born, not-become, not-made, not-compounded (condition). Monks, if that not-born, not-become, not-made, not-compounded (condition) were not, no escape from the born, become, made, compounded (condition) has been known here. But, monks, since there is a not-born, not-become, not-made, not-compounded (condition), therefore an escape from the born, become, made, compounded (condition) is known. (*Udāna* 80; see also Johansson 1969, ch. 12)

Granting also the comparability of the isolated soul in Sānkhya and the Universal Self, I can discern no positive ascriptions of the state of *kaivalya*. For since not only sorrow but also bliss are dependent upon association with the natural world (i.e., with *prakriti*), the released soul has no further experiences. As Hiriyanna indicates (1932:293),

The ideal is kaivalya or aloofness from prakṛti and all its transformations, which is quite in consonance with the pessimistic attitude of the doctrine. It is also termed apavarga, for the self in that state *escapes* from the realm of suffering. But no positive bliss is associated with it. The self not only has no pain or pleasure in that condition; it is also without knowledge, for it has not the means, *viz*. the buddhi and its accessories, wherewith to know.

Elucidation of the paradox may be facilitated by the recognition that the *Bhagavad-Gītā*, the writings of Shankara, Mahāyāna Buddhism, Eckhart, Pseudo-Dionysius, Gregory

Palamas, etc. contain elements of theistic belief, i.e. notions of a deity (or deities) who can be an active agent in the process of salvation, and with whom individuals may enter into a personal relationship. (This is not to deny that there are theistic elements in both Theravāda Buddhism and in Sānkhya. Nevertheless, the existence of a God [or Gods] is ultimately irrelevant to liberation in both these systems. Sānkhya is atheistic in so far as we are talking of the *Sāmkhyakārikās* [see Larson 1969:132–135].) Thus, in those systems in which theism has a prominent aspect, the positive aspects of the paradox are apparent. Stace's framework is unable to take this into account, whereas, by contrast the Smartian analysis of the numinous (theistic) strand provides a most adequate explanation for those contexts in which the vacuum-plenum paradox is evident; the positive aspect is provided by the numinous strand, the negative aspect by the mystical strand.

Stace's failure to recognize the possibility that the positive aspects of the paradox are based on theism derives from his philosophical critique of it. A basic presupposition of his conceptual framework is the methodological postulate that the reign of law in nature is a universal law. He writes, '. . . all macroscopic existences and events occurring in the space-time world are explicable without exception by natural causes' (1961:22–23). It follows from this that theism is ruled out *a priori* (ibid., p. 23): 'The naturalistic principle forbids us to believe that there ever occur interruptions in the natural working of events or capricious interventions by a supernatural being.'

Thus, for Stace (ibid., p. 25), the positive aspect of the vacuum-plenum paradox can *only* be attributed to an 'object' which does not intervene in the causal nexus but rather 'underlies' it (the Universal Self). Nevertheless, as is apparent from our analysis of the theistic experience, the notions of creativity, activity, and personality would seem to be far more applicable in a context in which there is the postulation of a connection between the cosmos and a 'supra'-cosmic deity. To this extent, the vacuum-plenum paradox cannot be seen as related *only* to the mystical experience but rather to the interweaving of mystical and theistic modes of expression.

In the chapter entitled 'Pantheism, Dualism, and Monism', Stace compares and contrasts three different ways of interpreting the mystical experience. The nature of these is defined by Stace in the following way (1961:219):

Dualism is the view that the relation between God and the world, including the relation between God and the individual self when in a state of union, is a relation of pure otherness or difference with no identity. Monism is the view that the relation is pure identity with no difference. Pantheism is the view that it is identity in difference.

Stace maintains that neither dualism nor monism are correct interpretations of mystical experience. We may begin by considering his critique of the dualist interpretation.

Stace argues that there are two main problems with the dualist interpretation. Firstly, the dualist interpretation distorts the key phenomenological characteristic of mystical experience, namely, that it is an undifferentiated experience beyond all multiplicity. Thus, he argues, an interpretation which asserts any dichotomy between God and the soul contradicts the nuclear characteristic of mystical experience. Secondly, he maintains that the dualist interpretation arises from almost exclusive emphasis on introspective experience. Stace considers that this is because, in the dualist interpretation, there is between the soul and God an affinity of psychic elements — of will, emotion, and cognition — and that such an affinity cannot be applied to the extrovertive experience since 'it does not make sense to speak of a resemblance between the volitions, emotions, and cognitions of pieces of wood and stone' (1961:235).

Nevertheless, if it is the case that a dualist interpretation directly contradicts the nature of the experience (and this necessitates the bracketing out of the question posed in an earlier chapter as to the possibility of theistic mystical experiences), the question arises why it is the case that dualist interpretations are preferred.

Stace explains this by postulating that mystics (especially those of Judaism, Christianity, and Islam) are forced into this position by ecclesiastical authorities:

There is something in the theistic religions which causes their theologians — who usually have no mystical experience and are only intellectuals — to outlaw as a heresy any tendency to monism or pantheism. The mystics have for the most part been pious men, obedient to the constituted authorities in the religion in which they have been raised. They humbly submit all their conclusions to the judgement of the Church or whatever the institutional authority in their religion may be. (Stace 1961:234)

There are two problems with this account of the reasons for dualistic interpretations. The first of these turns upon Stace's notion of the crucial distinction between mystical experience and its interpretation. While he admits that the distinction between experience and interpretation is hard to draw, nevertheless, he maintains that 'interpretation' may be understood to mean, '. . . anything which the conceptual intellect *adds to* the experience for the purpose of understanding it, whether what is added is only classificatory concepts, or a logical inference, or an explanatory hypothesis' (ibid., p. 37, my italics).

The implication of this passage, and of the preceding one when considered in its light, is that interpretation only occurs *post eventu*. That is to say, the experience itself is a *tabula rasa* which is only subsequently written upon. This is substantially the same notion of the relation between experience and interpretation used by Smart in his critique of Zaehner. We shall develop the point at some depth later and therefore, suffice it to say at the moment that this notion ignores other possible relationships between mystical experience and its interpretation. Thus, for example, it may be postulated that 'ramifications' may enter into accounts of mystical experience, not only because of retrospective interpretation, but also because a mystic's beliefs, practices, expectations, etc. may colour the experience itself. That is to say, an extant interpretative framework is a constitutive factor of the mystical experience. This means that we ought to take into account the possibility that the interpretation of mystical experience is influenced by a set of social and cultural factors far more complex than mere ecclesiastical pressure. The second problem with Stace's critique of dualism is that the postulation of ecclesiastical pressure cannot explain the presence of dualist interpretations within the Indian tradition in which no such pressure exists.[7] If we take Madhva, a pious Vaishnavite, as an Indian example of such dualist metaphysics, then the prime motive for his dualism would appear to be, not ecclesiastical pressure, but rather the necessity of an attack upon Advaita Vedānta which was perceived by Madhva as a direct threat to the theistic element within Vaishnavism. This also amounts to the possibility of course that the crucial element in Madhva's system is not the mystical but rather the theistic.[8] But this possibility is in itself sufficient to show the untenability of ecclesiastical pressure as the primary causative factor in dualist interpretation.

To turn to monism, Stace holds the view that it may take either of two forms, atheistic or acosmic. Atheistic monism means that nothing exists apart from the universe and that God is merely a name for the collection of finite objects which comprise the universe. Taken in this way, Stace (1961:237) is quite right in his assertion that it is of little philosophical interest. By contrast, acosmic monism is that type which holds that the universe as separate from God (or the Godhead) does not exist, that God alone as an undifferentiated unity is real. The Advaita Vedānta of Gaudapāda and Shankara is the paradigm of this type.

Stace argues that this type of monism must end in nonsense. This is because no reasonable answer can be given to the question, 'how does the theory explain the appearance of the multiplicity of finite objects?' (Stace 1961:237) There is no doubt that Stace has criticized the major weakness for any monistic scheme such as Advaita Vedānta. The dilemma for the Advaita school may be expressed in this way: Either, one must deny the unity, immutability, simplicity, and permanence of the Absolute (Brahman) by asserting that there is a *real* transformation of the Absolute into the multiplicity of phenomena in which case explanation of the appearance of the multiplicity of finite objects can be facilitated;

or, one may retain the unity, immutability, etc. of the Absolute
and remain agnostic regarding the nature and origin of illusion
(Sherrard 1974:413). The latter is the position taken by Advaita
Vedānta. The former is the position adopted by the Vishisht-
advaita Vedānta of Rāmānuja who rejected the monism of
Advaita in part because of its inability to resolve the question of
the origin of the 'appearance' of phenomena (for example, see
Rāmānuja's commentary on the *Vedāntasūtras*, 1.4.27).

Similarly, Stace would wish to maintain that the correct form
of monism is that in which the world is both identical with God
and distinct from (that is, not identical with) God. This relationship constitutes, according to Stace, the pantheistic paradox. In
Stace's opinion, dualism errs in that it fails to recognize the
former of the two alternatives, and monism errs in being unable
to assert the latter alternative.

Thus, for Stace, pantheism or the realization of identity in
difference is the true interpretation. Stace is quite correct in his
claim that this interpretation is present in the Upanishads (see, for
example, *Mundaka* Upanishad, 1.1.6; the seeds of acosmic monism are, however, also present, see *Brihadāranyaka* Upanishad,
III.8). I find it also quite explicitly not only in Eckhart, but also
in Islamic mystics such as Ibn 'Arabī (Corbin 1969, ch. 3) and Ibn
Tufayl (Hawi 1974, ch. 7), and (in so far as these can be considered as within a mystical tradition) in Spinoza (Parkinson
1977) and Hegel (Copleston 1976). Furthermore, the philosophy
of Plotinus, upon which ultimately depends both the Christian
and Islamic streams of mysticism, is quite clearly pantheistic in
Stace's sense of the term (see, for example, *Enneads*, 2.9.3.8;
4.8.6.12-13; 4.8.6.1-3; also Rist 1967; for the influence of Neo-
platonism on Islamic thought, see Fakhry 1970:32-44; and for the
influence of Plotinus on Christian mysticism, see Underhill
1977:82-113). However, if Stace's postulation of pantheism as the
true interpretation of the mystical experience is to be acceptable,
it will need to be shown that the utterances of mystics of both
introvertive and extrovertive types, when considered *without doctrinal ramifications* (whether arising from ecclesiastical pressure

or from some other means), give support to the mystical experience as being in essence one of identity in difference.

In the section entitled 'Justification of Pantheism', Stace initially examines the notion of the infinity of God. He argues that
this notion means 'that outside which, and other than which,
there is nothing' (1961:242). That is to say, the world is contained
in God. He points out that it is this notion that explains the
relation between mystical experience and pantheism in that it
gives us 'the monistic half of the pantheistic paradox, the identity
of the world and God' (ibid., p. 242). It is not at all clear whether
Stace, at this juncture, in referring to relations between God and
the world, is including therein relations between God and the
individual soul. Let us presume that he is talking of the relation
between God and the world exclusive of the relation between God
and the soul. If this is the case, then he is arguing that the *extro-*
vertive experience provides the monistic half of the pantheistic
paradox. That is to say, he is asserting that it is the absence of
multiplicity in the world and a recognition of its oneness as apprehended in the extrovertive experience which provides the identity relation within the pantheistic paradox.

However, if Stace is arguing thusly, then this conflicts with his
analysis of the characteristics of the extrovertive experience.
While commenting on the experience of 'N.M.', Stace remarks in
an earlier section (1961:72, my italics),

All-important is the experience that all the objects manifested, or possessed, *one*
life, while at the same time they 'did not cease to be individuals'. *This is the*
essence of the extrovertive type of experience.

Similarly, he earlier describes the major characteristic of extrovertive mysticism as,

The unifying vision, expressed abstractly by the formula 'All is One'. The One
is . . . perceived through the physical senses, *in or through the multiplicity of*
objects. (ibid., p. 79, my italics)

Thus, on the one hand, Stace appears to be asserting that the extrovertive experience leads to a monistic interpretation (in which, by his definition, the multiplicity of objects is illusory) in the section dealing with the conceptual justification of pantheism. On the other hand, his phenomenological analysis of the extrovertive experience asserts that its major characteristic is the seeing of the One *through the many* which entails that the many are *real* and not illusory. These different perspectives on the extrovertive experience are incompatible.

That Stace is referring to the extrovertive experience in his discussions of relations between God and the world is moreover demanded by the fact that it is above all in the introvertive experience that he wishes to argue that the notion of identity in difference is apparent. Now, to be sure, as I have indicated above, there is no dearth of mystical utterances evincing the notion of identity in difference. But the crucial question is whether these utterances actually do reflect the mystical experience itself. Stace fully appreciates the point that the most effective means of demonstrating that pantheism and the mystical experience are inextricably and ineluctably connected is to show that there are pantheistic *experiences* and not merely pantheistic *interpretations*. To this end, he sets out to eliminate the gap between experience and interpretation. Consonant with his critique of dualist interpretations as being the result of ecclesiastical pressure, Stace's method amounts to the elimination of those aspects of mystical interpretation which would appear to be derived from such pressure.

In order to demonstrate that there are such pantheistic experiences, Stace examines the following extract from Eckhart: 'Does she [i.e. the soul] find herself or not? . . . God has left her one little point from which to get back to herself . . . and know herself creature' (Stace 1961:244).

He points out that although the soul loses itself in the Divine unity (the identity), nevertheless, 'the "little point" is the element of difference' (ibid.). Similarly, in the passage from Suso — 'in this merging of itself in God the spirit passes away and yet not wholly' (ibid.) — Stace argues that the actual experience of identity in difference is evidenced. Although, as Stace points out, Suso goes on to interpret his experience in an overtly *dualistic* way, he maintains that the 'yet not wholly' is a direct reflection of the experience, whereas the dualistic interpretation is that of a dutiful son of the church who has left direct experience behind.

The following problems arise from this account. Firstly, Stace is arguing that the *actual experience* manifests identity in difference. However, his phenomenological analysis of the introvertive experience purported to show that the major characteristic of such experience was its absolute non-duality. That is to say, undifferentiated unity was proposed as the essence of the introvertive experience. There is then a *prima-facie* incompatibility between Stace's two notions of the introvertive experience. If he wishes to assert the absolute non-duality of the experience, he is forced to the position of maintaining that such expressions as 'the little point' are not expressive of the experience itself but are part of the interpretation. Alternatively, if he wishes to assert that identity in difference is the essence of the introvertive experience, he is forced to relinquish his postulation of non-duality or undifferentiated unity as the universal core of mysticism. The incompatibility noted above between the conceptual justification of pantheism and the phenomenological analysis of the extrovertive experience is repeated with reference to the introvertive experience. That is to say, in the earlier sections of *Mysticism and Philosophy*, Stace analyses the extrovertive experience as evincing identity in difference, while in later sections he argues that the extrovertive experience provides the monistic half of the pantheistic paradox. By contrast, he initially characterizes the introvertive experience as one of undifferentiated unity and only subsequently argues that it is an *actual* experience of identity in difference. Indeed, he maintains (1961:132) in his phenomenological analysis of the introvertive experience that the extrovertive experience finds its completion in the introvertive precisely because it is only in the latter that the identity in difference of the former is completely obliterated in an experience of total unity.

What are the corollaries for Stace's account in the light of the above discussion? The possible corollaries are as follows:
(i) That introvertive experiences are experiences of identity in difference and not of undifferentiated unity;
(ii) that introvertive experiences are experiences of undifferentiated unity and that identity in difference is merely an interpretation of such experiences;
(iii) that there are both experiences of undifferentiated unity and experiences of identity in difference.
Determination of extrovertive experience may be seen as dependent upon acceptance of one of these. We shall consider these in the order (iii), (ii), and (i).

We have seen above that Stace makes much of two passages from Eckhart and Suso which he claims are evidence of identity in difference. By way of contrast, we shall consider two other passages. The first, from the writings of Eckhart, reads as follows:

The soul should be independent and should not want anything and then it would attain godly stature by reason of likeness [to him]. Nothing makes for unity as much as likeness. For God, too, is independent and needs nothing. In this way the soul enters the unity of the Holy Trinity but it may become even more blessed by going further, to the barren Godhead, of which the Trinity is a revelation. In this barren Godhead, activity has ceased and therefore the soul will be most perfect when it is thrown into the desert of the Godhead, where both activity and forms are no more, so that it is sunk and lost in this desert *where its identity is destroyed* and it has no more to do with things than it had before it existed. (Blakney 1941:200–201, my italics)

The second passage is from the writings of Suso (*Buchlein der Wahrheit*, ch. 4, quoted in Underhill 1930:424, my italics) and describes the mystical union:

'Lord tell me', says the Servitor, 'what remains to a blessed soul which has wholly renounced itself'. Truth says, 'When the good and faithful servant enters into the joy of his Lord, he is inebriated by the riches of the house of God; for he feels, in an ineffable degree, that which is felt by an inebriated man. He forgets himself, he is no longer conscious of his selfhood; he disappears and loses himself in God, and becomes one spirit with him as a drop of water which is drowned in a great quantity of wine. For even as such a drop disappears, taking the colour and the taste of the wine, so it is with those who are in the full possession of blessedness. . . . If it were otherwise, *if there remained in the man some human thing that was not absorbed, those words of Scripture which say that God must be all in all would be false'*.

I have quoted these passages at length to make two points. Firstly, in both passages, the relationship between the self and the Godhead is said to be one of complete identity. And secondly, therefore, neither Eckhart nor Suso provide evidence that identity in difference is part of the mystical experience; on the contrary, the clear implication is that the experiences about which both Eckhart and Suso are speaking at this point are experiences of undifferentiated unity, albeit expressed in theistic terms. Thus, unless Suso and Eckhart are speaking of different sorts of experiences in the respective passages, and this seems highly unlikely, then corollary (iii) must be denied. To be sure, there remains the possibility that there are other experiences of identity in difference apart from the purported ones of Eckhart and Suso. However, in so far as we are speaking of these two mystics, the rejection of corollary (iii) is necessary.

Turning to corollary (i), we may note that verification of this proposition would not only entail the denial that the above two passages are expressive of experiences of undifferentiated unity, but would also necessitate demonstrating that the notion of identity in difference is evident in the writings of such a tradition as Theravāda Buddhism. It is to be noted that in Stace's elaboration of identity in difference he makes reference only to passages from mystics who operate within traditions which have theistic elements and fails to advert to Theravāda Buddhism at all.

In order to investigate this possibility, however, we shall briefly turn again to the Theravādin tradition. More specifically, we need to ask whether in Theravāda Buddhism there may be said to be an X which is both identical with yet different from a God (or Universal Self). Clearly, however, in the asking of this question, the question is dissolved. For, with respect to Theravāda, denying as it does the concept of a self (see Chapter 3, note 6) and denying also the concept of a Universal Self, the question is a nonsensical one.

Stace could perhaps maintain that Theravāda Buddhism, in not taking cognizance of the apprehension of difference in the mystical experience, has misinterpreted it. That is to say, Stace could argue that Theravāda Buddhists do experience identity in difference but their interpretation is in error. Such a claim would however be difficult to substantiate, and this for three reasons. Firstly, from an examination of the Pali texts, particularly those dealing with the nature of *Nibbāna*, it would be difficult to show that the Theravādin experience is one of identity in difference (for a comprehensive account of the Pali texts dealing with *nibbāna*, see Johansson 1969). Secondly, Stace has offered no criteria by means of which he can argue that an error of interpretation has occurred in Theravāda Buddhism. His criticisms of monism and dualism are not applicable since Theravāda is neither monistic (because it asserts the reality of the world),[9] nor dualistic (because it denies the existence of an absolute deity) (von Glasenapp 1970:35). Thirdly, in his discussion of Theravāda Buddhism, he rather surprisingly maintains that even the notion of a pure self emptied of its empirical contents is an interpretation, and, that 'what is actually experienced is simply the unity' (Stace 1961:125). From this, it follows that the 'difference' aspect of the pantheistic paradox cannot be a part of the experience itself (as Stace maintains in his justification of pantheism) since the aspect of difference is totally dependent upon there *actually* being an entity pertaining to the individual such as a soul. This point leads to a consideration of the second corollary above.

Our second corollary agrees with both Smart's analysis of mystical experience and with Stace's phenomenological analysis of the introvertive experience. We have seen earlier that for Stace, the interpretation of mystical experience is always retrospective to the experience and that dualist interpretations are due to ecclesiastical pressure. From this perspective, it is not at all difficult to see that such expressions as 'the little point' and 'yet not wholly' are expressive of the experience itself, for it is unlikely that the occurrence of such doctrinally unramified expressions are the result of, for example, ecclesiastical pressure. However, if it is the case that the whole cultural set of the mystic enters into his interpretation, then such expressions as 'the little point' and 'yet not wholly' may be seen in a number of different lights. They may, for example, be seen as the reflections of a cultural set in which the status of the Creator over against the creature is a central point and the assertion of the identity of God and the soul an impious impossibility. This would certainly fit Suso's gloss on the 'yet not wholly' passage (Stace 1961:244).[10] Alternatively, they may be seen more broadly as the reflection of an Occidental set which takes the reality of this world as a basic presupposition in the development of any Absolutist metaphysic. This presupposition which, within a mystical schema, may be traced at least as far back as Plotinus,[11] dovetails well with a theistic schema which entails a physical realism. Thus, from this viewpoint, 'the little point' may be seen as a recognition on the part of Eckhart that while from the perspective of mystical consciousness all is identity, from the perspective of the every-day consciousness in which, to paraphrase Eckhart, the soul finds herself subsequent to the mystical experience, there *must be* difference. Thus, while the mystical experience demands identity, the realist presupposition demands at least some relative (yet not absolute) difference. A similar position is reflected in the writings of Ibn Tufayl. Thus, according to S. S. Hawi, when Ibn Tufayl affirms that God both is and is not identical with the soul, then the affirmation and negation are operating on two different modes and levels. Hawi writes (1974:218),

The fact of the matter is that Hayy understood and contended that the world is identical with God only during his utter annihilation. God, through *extreme subjectivism (intuitive method)* appears to be identical with the world. . . . But such an awareness of undiluted pantheism is of a *different order than the sensible world* of which our language is part; such being the case, the expression of this awareness by *an objective sensible* language can only be effected metaphorically by saying that He is and He is not identical with the world.

In essence, therefore, for Ibn Tufayl the notion of identity in difference arises from the necessity of interweaving an ontology arising from the mystical experience of undifferentiated unity with an ontology arising from the evidence of the sensory realm. For Eckhart, Ibn Tufayl, and Suso, identity in difference is not part of the mystical experience but part of its interpretation.

In summary, we have seen that neither corollaries (iii) nor (i) are adequate as accounts of mystical experience, and that, on the contrary, our discussion of corollary (ii) renders it the most plausible proposition for us to adopt in the light of our critique of Stace.

In this chapter, I have argued that Stace's inability to take theism seriously, his failure to come to grips with the modes of expression in Theravāda and Sānkhya, and his unsubtle model of the relationship between mystical experience and interpretation render his philosophical arguments problematical. Our discussion has however given credence to his claim that there is a mystical experience of undifferentiated unity, and, in so far as Stace recognizes the unity of interior mystical experience, he is in agreement with Ninian Smart. Thus, against Zaehner, both would agree that interior mystical experience admits of no varieties.

We have seen also, that Stace's philosophical exclusion of theism, and his subsequent inability to consider the theistic strand in an account of mystical experience renders his analysis dubious at a number of points. Furthermore, while Smart excludes panenhenic experience from consideration, both Zaehner and Stace agree on the necessity for including panenhenic or extrovertive mystical experience in their analyses. During the course of this chapter however, I have suggested the possibility of distinguishing two modes of panenhenic expression, that which arises as the result of spontaneous extrovertive experience, and that which arises as the result of reflecting upon the world of every-day consciousness subsequent to an introvertive experience. Furthermore, I have suggested as a general methodological principle that, except where there is autobiographical evidence to the contrary, and of course, where there *is* evidence of introvertive experience, that panenhenic modes of expression be taken as reflections on the relationship of that experience to the multiple and diverse realm of every-day consciousness.

In essence, therefore, our analysis has generated the likelihood of there being introvertive experiences of undifferentiated unity, panenhenic experiences of a spontaneous kind (though no evidence that these are of importance in doctrinal schemes has yet been accepted), and religious experiences of a theistic kind. In chapter three of this essay, we noted in broad outline the nature of numinous experience as outlined by Rudolf Otto. We shall now return to the writings of Rudolf Otto to consider his analysis of the relationship between numinous experience, and introvertive and extrovertive mystical experience.

5

The Mystical, the Numinous, and Metaphysics:
The Theory of Rudolf Otto

There is no doubt that the central contribution of Rudolf Otto to the study of religion, his analysis of the numinous experience, has permeated the philosophy of religion to the extent that no consideration of religious experience is possible without at least a reference to his work. In the light of his influence, it is perhaps surprising that there have been very few major works upon Otto in the English-speaking world which attempt to present the thought of Otto in its full complexity. (The only two to my knowledge are Davidson 1947, and to a lesser extent Moore 1938.)

It is probably because of this dearth of material, that those references to Otto which appear in numerous articles, anthologies, etc., have invariably emphasized the *theistic* implications of Otto's writings, and in particular, of *The Idea of the Holy*, the book for which Otto is justly most renowned. Certainly, the theistic implications of Otto's writings have been validly delineated; indeed, I have attempted to do just this in an earlier chapter of this study. Nevertheless, the emphasis upon these has been so great that interpretations of Rudolf Otto's writings have been in consequence, one-sided and unbalanced.

In this chapter, it is hoped that there is the beginning of a corrective to this one-sided emphasis upon the theistic ramifications of Otto's thought. Hence, by means of an exposition of Otto's understanding of the mystical experience, and a consideration of the relationship between this experience and the category of the numinous experience, I shall attempt to show that for Otto, the numinous experience may be conceptualized, not only in theistic terms, but in trans-theistic and non-theistic terms. Thereby, we shall hope to cast some fresh light on the possible relation of mystical and numinous experience. Furthermore, this will enable us to delineate some problems regarding Otto's theory of religious truth.

There can be no question that interpreters of Rudolf Otto's writings are correct when they maintain that for Otto, all religions are based on the numinous experience, the experience of a *Mysterium, Tremendum et Fascinans*. However, as indicated above, it is often presumed that according to Otto the numinous experience is invariably and inexorably couched in theistic terms. Examples of this presumption may be derived from numerous and varied writings in the philosophy of religion. To take but two of these: In a context in which he is speaking of the relation between the world and God, and subsequent to an outline of Otto's major thesis, R. W. Hepburn (1971:173), asks the question,

Could numinous experience be taken as an actual privileged awareness of the world as related to God, of God as related to the world?

In this passage, Hepburn is questioning whether numinous experience is the source for the tenacity of the cosmological argument in the history of the philosophy of religion. For our purposes, it is sufficient to note that for Hepburn, the numinous experience *is* conceptualized in theistic terms, in terms of the relation between world and God, between the created and the creator. At no point does Hepburn indicate that for Otto, as we shall see, the numinous experience may be conceptualized in quite different terms. To be sure, Hepburn's error is not all that earth-shattering and, in the context of the question as to whether religious experience grants privileged access to religious truth, does not affect his analysis. It does, however, give evidence of the almost unquestioned acceptance of the assumption indicated above. Of more importance is our next example.

That for Otto, the numinous experience is pre-eminently conceptualized in theistic terms is not only accepted by Ninian Smart but is also used as an argument against Otto's purported position. Thus, speaking of the relation between the aspects of *Mysterium, Tremendum* and *Fascinans*, he remarks (1964b: 110–111),

Though a man, when confronted with the Holy, thinks of it as wholly other — there is, so to speak, a great gulf fixed between sinful man and the holy deity which he confronts — nevertheless he is drawn towards it.

This connection of the numinous experience with its conceptualization in theistic terms leads Smart to the following conclusion (ibid., pp. 112–113):

Otto has certainly illuminated an important type of religious experience. But perhaps he has not adequately represented the nature of mysticism — that is, the quest through contemplation for inner insight.

The implication of the word 'type' in the first sentence of the above passage from Smart is that Otto has omitted the category of mystical experience from his analysis of religious experience. The implication of the remainder of the passage is however that Otto, although representing the nature of mysticism in some (unexplained) sense, has not adequately done so. That there are two major types of religious experience, the numinous and the mystical, and that each is completely unique and non-reducible to the other is, as we have seen in Chapter three, a major presupposition of Smart's own analysis of religions. However we interpret the above passage, if Smart's criticism of Otto is to be valid, the following questions need to be resolved. Firstly, what is the relationship for Otto between the numinous and the mystical experience? And secondly, and consequent upon the first, must the numinous experience be conceptualized in theistic terms?

Otto's major consideration of mystical experience is contained in his comparative analysis of Meister Eckhart and Shankaracharya, *Mysticism East and West* (1932). In this book, Otto, like Stace (in fact, Stace is primarily dependent on Otto's analysis), argues that there are two types of mystical experience which may be inferred from mystical writings in general, and from the writings of Eckhart and Shankara in particular. These are designated the Mysticism of Introspection (the Inward Way) and the Mysticism of Unifying Vision (the Outward Way). Before proceeding to a more detailed examination of these, it will be useful to indicate the basic difference between them. As with the analysis offered by Stace so also with Otto's, the Mysticism of Introspection turns away from the world of things external to the self and looks 'within' for the inmost depths of the self. By contrast, the Mysticism of Unifying Vision looks out upon the world of finitude and multiplicity and, within the finite perceives the infinite, within the temporal perceives the eternal, and within the multiplicity perceives a unity. We shall turn our attention primarily to this latter form.

Otto maintains that three 'logically' ascending steps can be discerned in the Mysticism of Unifying Vision. At the lowest stage, the perceived world is transfigured in a unity in which space and time are transcended, in which all is one and one is all. Concurrent with this vision of the identity in difference of the world external to the perceiver of it, the perceiver recognizes that he himself is part of this unity. That is to say, the distinction between the perceiver and the perceived collapses. Otto quotes Plotinus to this effect (1932:67):

He who has allowed the beauty of that world (seen in ideal unity) to penetrate his soul goes away no longer a mere observer. For the object perceived and the perceiving soul are no longer two things separated from one another, but the perceiving soul has (now) within itself the perceived object.

While mystical intuition may remain at this lowest stage, Otto maintains that it can progress to a higher. In the lowest stage, the unity and multiplicity are a *coincidentia oppositorum*. In the second stage, however, emphasis is placed upon the unity which now becomes conceptualized as 'the One'. 'The One' is the substantial, the permanent, and the constant 'behind' or 'beyond' the changing and fleeting many:

In relation to the many it [the One] becomes the subject in so far as it unifies, comprehends and bears the many. It is in fact its essence, being, existence. Already at this point the One concentrates attention upon itself, draws the value of the many to itself, silently becoming that which is and remains the real value behind the many. (Otto 1932:68)

With respect to the relation of the One to the many at this second stage, Otto is fairly obscure. He appears to argue that, in so far as this relation is rationally determinable, such conceptualization may take either of two forms. Firstly, where this stage of mystical intuition is grafted upon theism, 'the One' is called 'God'. In this case, the relationship between God and the world is a causal one, the indeterminable non-rational mystical relationship being conceptualized in the rational category of cause and effect. Thus, Otto appears to maintain that a conceptualization in terms of a transcendent Creator over against an ontologically real creation may be generated. Shadows of theistic numinosity are quite clearly evident. Alternatively, the notion of immanence may be generated whereby the One 'conditions' the many in the sense of lying at the basis of the many as its principle. In other words, either a transcendent One or an immanent One may be generated. Or, both may be combined as in the *Isha* Upanishad (5): 'It moves and It moves not; It is far and It is near; It is within all this and It is also outside all this.'

If these alternative conceptualizations are not taken as final, the ascension to the third stage may be made. In this stage, 'the One' appears over against the many as the only truly Real. Otto writes (1932:70–71),

> The many, at first identical with the One, comes into conflict with it, and disappears. It disappears either by sinking down into the indivisible One, as with Eckhart, or by becoming the obscuring veil of the One, the illusion of māyā in Avidyā, as with Śankara.

Again, Otto's exposition of this third stage, since it is extremely succinct, is by no means clear. Nevertheless, his intention appears to be that the two conceptualizations of the second stage, transcendent creator deity or immanent One, may be transcended by a conceptualization in which, since only the One exists, a cosmic idealism is generated. Thus the immanence of the One in things is transcended in the case of Shankara by the assertion of the sole existence of the Godhead, Brahman. As we would expect from our discussion of the realist strand in Plotinian-based mysticism in the last chapter, for Eckhart the One remains immanent. Nevertheless, beyond the immanent One, there rises for Eckhart the completely transcendent One, 'the silent void of the Godhead'.

There are a number of features of the above analysis which are worth some elaboration in the light of our discussions in earlier chapters of this essay. Firstly, Otto's examples of the Outward Way all fall prey to our previously enunciated autobiographical principle. That is to say, there is no evidence adduced by Otto that the panenhenic modes of expression quoted by him are the result of panenhenic experience. Further, let us consider two passages adduced by Otto as examples of the transition from the second to the third stage. The first passage, from Eckhart, deals with the unity beneath the multiplicity of the world:

So long as the soul still beholds a divided world, all is not well with it. So long as anything separate looks in or peeps out, so long there is not yet unity. . . . The soul is troubled so long as it perceives created things in their separateness. All that is created, or that is capable of being created, is nought. But that (viz. the thing itself beheld in its ratio ydealis) is apart from all creation, indeed from all possibility of creation. Because it is something united, something without relation to another. (Otto 1932:77–78)

According to Otto, there is in the following passage (ibid., p. 78) a transition to a higher stage of mystical consciousness:

So long as the soul beholds forms (nāmarūpe, mūrti), even though she beheld an angel, or herself as something formed: so long is there imperfection in her. Yes, indeed, should she even behold God (as separate), in so far as He is with form and number in the Trinity: so long is there imperfection in her. Only when all that is formed is cast off from the soul, and she sees the Eternal-One alone, then the pure essence of the soul feels the naked, unformed essence of the divine Unity — more, still, a Beyond-Being. O wonder of wonders, what a noble endurance is that where the essence of the soul suffers no suggestion or shadow of difference even in thought or in name. There she entrusts herself alone to the One, free from all multiplicity and difference, in which all limitation and quality is lost and is one.

Otto is quite correct in his claim that there is a movement in these passages from unity in diversity to absolutely un-differentiated unity. The question is however, whether this logical development in any way is a reflection of experiential develop-ment. Now, to be sure, these passages can be interpreted so that they fit Otto's model of the mysticism of unifying vision. Yet, it is perhaps fruitful to consider them in the light of the model we have been developing in this study. According to this model, panenhenic modes of expression are interpretations of the exter-nal world of multiplicity subsequent to the interior experience of undifferentiated unity. From this perspective, the second passage is a description of consciousness turning inwards, casting off all external forms, consciousness of itself, consciousness of any duality (even of that between the soul and God), until there is reached an undifferentiated unity 'free from all multiplicity and difference'. Certainly, this psychological experience of undifferentiated unity is given ontological status as the One. But, this arises from the reflection upon the seeming ultimacy of the experience in its relation to the world of multiplicity, in terms of the underlying Plotinian philosophy. Indeed for Plotinus too, the unitive experience provides a guarantee experientially of the demands of abstract thought. As E. R. Dodds points out (1960:6–7) with reference to Plotinus,

> The term *to 'EV* [the One] was given in the tradition; the concept can be reached, and by Plotinus most often *is* reached, through a purely philosophical argument, an argument from the existence of the relative to the necessity of an Absolute. . . . What the experience of unification seems to do is to give the assurance that the outcome of this regressive dialectic is no hollow abstraction, that the minus signs of the *via negativa* are in reality plus signs. . . . It is, as it were, the experimental verification of the abstract proposition that the One is the Good; for to experience unification is to experience the highest of all forms of life.

We may therefore suggest that the first passage above is evi-dence of this reflection upon the world subsequent to the unitive experience. Here is evidenced the necessity of perceiving in the external world that which has been apprehended within. As Evelyn Underhill (1930:102) writes of mystics in general,

The mystic assumes — because he tends to assume an orderly basis for things — that there is a relation, an analogy, between this microcosm of man's self and the macrocosm of the world-self. Hence, his experience, the geography of the individual quest, appears to him good evidence of the geography of the Invisible.[1]

A number of clarificatory points need to be made at this stage of our argument. Firstly, there may appear to be some incompatibility between the passages from Dodds and Underhill quoted above. For, according to Dodds, the experience of undifferentiated unity reinforces the philosophical postulation of the One at the basis of multiplicity. On the other hand, according to Underhill, the mystical experience at the individual level *generates* the assertion of the macrocosmic One. In fact, there is no incompatibility. In order to illuminate this, it is necessary to digress a little.

It may be recalled that according to Stace, the Universal Self was apprehended in the introvertive mystical experience. We criticized this notion on the grounds that there was no necessity to postulate such a Universal Self and that, in the traditions of Sānkhya and Theravāda Buddhism, the mystical experience was related to the notions of individual *purusha* and *anatta* respectively. Yet, in those traditions in which there is a philosophical tradition of Absolutist thought, as in the Upanishadic and Neoplatonic traditions,[2] that which is apprehended in the mystical experience is expressed in terms of the One, the Universal Self, etc. Thus, Dodds is correct in his claim that the mystical experience reinforces any incipient tendencies towards philosophical absolutism. Indeed, the presence of absolutist tendencies together with the mystical experience is precisely that which brings about the panenhenic mode of expression. Inversely, the rejection of absolutist conceptions in Sānkhya and Theravāda Buddhism means the absence of panenhenic modes of expression in these traditions. Thus, to elaborate upon Underhill's statement, the mystic who develops a microcosm-macrocosm relation does so, not merely because of the assumption of an orderly basis for things, but because of his acceptance of a tradition of absolutist thought. In essence therefore, the presence of panenhenic modes of expression in the writings of some mystics, particularly those in the Upanishadic and Neo-platonic traditions, and the absence of such expression in others, especially those in the Theravādin and Sānkhyin traditions, is determined by the acceptance or rejection (whether overtly or not is of no consequence) of a tendency towards philosophical absolutism. There is, in other words, a complex interplay between the mystical experience of undifferentiated unity, and panenhenic modes of expression deriving from this, and connected with philosophical absolutism.

The point made above with reference to Theravāda Buddhism is perhaps deserving of a little more expansion. During the course of this study we have noted that both Stace and Otto claim that extrovertive mystical experience generates an ontology which deals with the 'One' which underlies the multiplicity of phenomena. On their models, therefore, the absence of such an ontology in e.g. Theravāda Buddhism can only be explained by them by the absence within Theravāda Buddhism of the extrovertive experience. I have suggested in this study that panenhenic modes of expression and therefore such ontologies are *better* explained by being viewed as reflection upon the multiplicity of phenomena subsequent to the introvertive experience by mystics within a tradition which is clearly or incipiently absolutist. I shall now attempt to indicate that reflection upon the world within the Buddhist tradition in relation to the mystical experience generates a substantively different mode of expression.

In a recent paper, Robert Gimmelo outlines the connection and distinction between mystical experience and meditational *praxis* within the Buddhist tradition. The essence of his argument is the establishing that meditation is a twofold discipline, and that the attainment of mystical experience is but a part:

On the one hand, there is what might be called a psychosomatic and affective component. This consists in acts of calming and concentrating the mind-body complex of the meditator, usually by the deliberate inducement of certain rarefied states of mind. These states are characterized by such qualities as ecstasy, joy, tranquillity, zest, equanimity, and one-pointedness of mind. These, in turn, precipitate or accompany extraordinary experiences in which the normal conditions of material, spatial, temporal, and mental existence seem suspended. Multiplicity, material resistance, distinction between subject and object, and the like — all vanish. . . . The purpose allegedly served by these practices is that of quelling, if not extirpating, desire, attachment, and other elements of the affective life. (Gimello 1978:187–188)

According to Gimello, such mystical experience is subsequently attended by an intellectual or analytic component of meditation (ibid., p. 188):

This consists in the meditatively intensified reflection upon the basic categories of Buddhist doctrine and in the application of them to the data of meditative experience. It is a form of discrimination, critical and sceptical in tone, which serves invariably to inhibit speculation or the formulation of views about the nature of reality. It does employ concepts — ideas like suffering, impermanence, emptiness, interdependence, etc. — but these it employs homoeopathically, as conceptual devices to counteract the mind's tendency to attach itself to concepts.

Let us consider an example of this dual discipline. In the *Uttarabhāvanākrama* of Kamalashīla, there is the following passage:

The yogin, fixing his mind on the physical form of the Tathāgata (i.e. the Buddha visualized in meditation) as it might appear to his senses, practises calming. He attends continually to the form of the Tathāgata, brilliant as refined gold, adorned with the major and minor marks (of a superior person). . . . Attracted by these qualities, the yogin quells all distraction and agitation and remains absorbed for as long as they appear to him distinctly, as if they were actually present. Then the yogin practises discernment by scrutinizing the coming and going of these reflections of the Tathāgata's form. He considers thus: Just as these reflections of the form of the Tathāgata neither come from anywhere nor go anywhere, are empty of own-being and devoid of self and its properties, so are all dharmas empty of own-being, without coming or going like a reflection, and lacking the features of an existent thing. (Quoted in Gimello 1978:184–185)

Thus, subsequent to the meditative experience of the Buddha, there is an intellectual reflection which serves to substantiate the doctrine that as all Buddhas are empty of substantial existence, so are all things thus empty. Within Buddhism therefore, and particularly Mahāyāna Buddhism, mystical experiences are used as reinforcers of particular Mahāyānist views about reality, specifically, that there are no valid views. As Gimello puts it (p. 193),

The only view confirmed by the Buddhist use of mystical experience is a reflexively negative one, namely the view that no views capture the nature of reality. . . . Likewise it is certain that Buddhists do not ontologize the contents of their mystical experiences, nor people the cosmos with mystical entities, since their very purpose in having them is to 'discern' their illusoriness.

As the mystical experience provided a guarantee of the demands of abstract thought for Plotinus, so also in Mahāyāna Buddhism, the mystical experience reinforces doctrinal views within this tradition. In both the Buddhist and the Neo-platonic traditions, the mystical experience is central. Yet in both, disparate views of the nature of the multiplicity of phenomena are generated.

In an article entitled 'Non-Being and *Mu*: The Metaphysical Nature of Negativity in the East and the West', Maseo Abe (1975) suggests reasons for this disparity in views between the Mahāyānist and Chinese view upon reality, and the Western view determined as it is by Platonic and Neo-platonic thought. There has been in the West, according to him, a fundamental thrust towards the granting of ontological priority to being as against non-being. This thrust is derived from both the major strands of Greek philosophy (through the ideas of *TO ON* and *ME ON*) and from the Christian tradition (through the assertion of *creatio ex nihilo*). These two have intertwined so that,

. . . since being prevails in the balance of being and non-being, to overcome the opposition between being and non-being means to approach Being with a capital B as the end. In the same way, to overcome the opposition between life and death means to reach Eternal Life, and to overcome the opposition between good and evil means to move toward Supreme Good. (Ibid., p. 183)[3]

By contrast, in the Mahāyānist tradition, both being and non-being are on equal footing. Thus, ontological priority is given neither to being nor non-being but rather to that which transcends and embraces both. This is particularly exemplified in Nāgārjuna's idea of *shūnyatā* (emptiness). Abe writes (1975:185),

Emptiness which is completely without form is freed from both being and non-being because 'non-being' is still a form as distinguished from 'being'. . . . Accordingly, Nāgārjuna's idea of the Middle Path does not simply indicate a midpoint between two extremes as the Aristotelian idea of *to meson* might suggest. Instead, it refers to the Way which transcends every possible duality including that of being and non-being, affirmation and negation.[4]

In the light of the two modes of thought thus outlined, a note upon the relation between these and the use of language within each may be fruitful. There are in effect two main ways of viewing the function of mystical language. The first of these is to see mystical language as attempting to describe that which is apprehended in mystical experience, that is, the 'subjective' or 'objective' reality (or both) therein. Thus, for example, Stace, Otto, and Evelyn Underhill all view mystical expression as descriptive language, in essence, as the mystic's vain attempt to put into words that which cannot be said because the Real is (subjectively) undifferentiated unity or (objectively) undifferentiated Being. There can be no denying that a large amount of mystical language is descriptive and this is particularly the case with those mystics operating within an ontology which is concerned with the relation between the One and the many, or with the nature of such a One or of Being. Otto outlines the dilemma for Eckhart and Shankara quite correctly (1932:22):

As pure Being (*esse*) God is completely 'fashionless', without 'How' or mode of being, neither this nor that, neither thus nor otherwise, just as Brahman is pure Being, is 'nirgunam' and 'neti, neti', absolutely 'One'. Therefore it is already as *esse purum* and *simplex* above all conceptions and conceptual differentiations, and so beyond all comprehending and apprehending (*akaranagocharam, avagmanogocharam*). For our comprehension is bound up with distinctions, with *genus* and *differentia specifica*.

There is however an alternative view of the relationship between mystical experience and its expression, a view exemplified predominantly in Mahāyāna Buddhism. According to F. J. Streng (1978:162), where a mystic assumes a transcendent awareness not oriented towards undifferentiated Being-itself, but rather towards a dynamic process of neither being nor not-being (*shūnyatā, tathata*),

... words do not function primarily as descriptions of something, but as a catalyst to free the mystic from a mental-emotional attachment to either being or non-being. The soteriological significance will be to cultivate an awareness of the emptiness of both form and non-form in which one is neither attached to, nor fearful of, either.

In essence, therefore, freedom must be gained from the illusoriness of all conceptualizations and perceptions, from the conceptual formation that has control of the individual's perceptions of reality, from the belief that there is a one-to-one correspondence between language and reality. Such freedom is not gained by sinking into undifferentiated bliss or views thereupon, but by *discerning* upon the basis of this the 'suchness' of all things. The suchness of all things is known through being non-attached to form without seeking the elimination of all form. Thus as Streng puts it (1978:162),

To know things as they are is not to know an undifferentiated ground or source of all things as set over against particular forms. Rather it is to be freed from 'clinging'. Both 'the state of all knowledge' ... and the constituents or properties of experienced things (*dharmas, skandhas*) are without self existent 'being' and thus incomparable, immeasurable and unthinkable. To be free one must not 'settle down' in form by grasping it; one must not even try to 'grasp' or settle down in all-knowledge by discriminating between form and a form-less reality.

This means that in Mahāyāna Buddhism, the goal is neither the attainment of mystical experience, nor the having of right views about the world. Rather, the goal is a certain orientation of the self in the world, a certain way of being and acting. (It can be argued that the same holds true for Theravāda Buddhism; see

Ling 1965.) The point of Buddhist meditation is not to obtain a certain 'thing', whether this be the bliss of undifferentiated unity or a right view about reality but to become a certain kind of man. Perhaps this element within Mahāyāna Buddhism is well exemplified in the 'Ten Oxherding Pictures' which depict in Zen Buddhism the stages on the way to enlightenment. The mystical experience is symbolized by an empty circle thereby pointing towards the transcending of all opposites in the undifferentiated experience. But, in the last two paintings, a wealth of detail returns. The last is entitled 'Return to the Market Place with Gift-Giving Hands' (reproductions and discussion of these paintings can be found in Suzuki 1960).

Perhaps sufficient has been said for us to make three points by way of summary: Firstly, that panenhenic modes of expression are not dependent upon extrovertive experience but rather upon a thrust towards Absolutism in traditions where there is an ontological priority of being over against non-being. Being (the One) lies behind the relative plane of being and not-being; secondly, that where being and non-being are considered as polar but ontically equal opposites, language is not merely descriptive of that which transcends both but evokes the existential realization of that which transcends and embraces both; thirdly, therefore, that mystical experience may support and reinforce both of these modes of thought, but does not necessitate either.

In contrast to the Mysticism of Unifying Vision, the Mysticism of Introspection rejects the external world for the 'inward' quest. For Eckhart, this inward quest leads to *das Gemüte*; for Shankara, to the *ātman*. Otto writes (1932:100),

Both ātman and soul must free themselves from the world which surrounds them. They must withdraw from the senses and from sense-impressions, without attachments to the objects of sense; they must free themselves from all outward objects as well as from objects of thought, and thus from all manifoldness, multiplicity, and difference.

Thus, in this unitive state, the distinction between knower, known, and knowing is obliterated, subject-object polarity is abrogated. According to Otto, for Eckhart, the soul 'has become completely one and is the One' (ibid.). That is to say, since the introspective state is one of undifferentiated unity, this may be taken as a state in which union or identity with the One is attained.

However, while the unitive experience *may be taken* as tantamount to union or identity with the One, the former may remain independent of such interpretation. There is no necessary connection between that which is apprehended in the two types of mystical experience outlined by Otto, nor does introspective mystical experience necessitate conceptualization in theistic or transtheistic terms. Thus, in contrast to Stace, Otto recognizes that if the introspective mystical experience is spoken of as the unification of the soul and God or as the identity in essence of the two, then it is impossible to account for those forms of mysticism in which theistic concepts are of little or no importance. For example, therefore, the introspective experience may be conceptualized in the non-theistic terms of the 'system' of Yoga:

We distinguish a Sa-iśvara-yoga and an an-iśvara-yoga, i.e. a yoga with God and a yoga without God. That the latter cannot be a unio mystica with God is clear; but in the former also God and union with Him is not the goal. There is here no effort after such a union, but after 'the isolation of the Ātman' for which God is merely an aid. (Otto 1932:160)

Thus, since the introspective mystical experience can be formulated in terms which do not include 'God' or one of its cognates, the 'Godhead' of Eckhart and the 'Brahman' of Shankara are not alternative names for the soul which has 'realized itself' in the introspective experience. That is, there is nothing ineluctable about the relation between the soul (or Ātman) and the Godhead (or Brahman); rather, the relationship between these is one of the synthesis of qualitatively different 'entities'. According to Otto (ibid., p. 102), it is this synthesizing of the Ātman-Brahman dichotomy that differentiates Shankara's speculation from that of Yoga:

Because it [Ātman] is also Brahman, something incalculable has been *added* to the Ātman, which is not contained in the kaivalyam of the ātman merely stripped of limitations. And exactly the same applies to Eckhart.

Accordingly, the One of the Mysticism of Unifying Vision (the Brahman, the Godhead) is combined with the One of the Mysticism of Introspection (the Ātman, the Soul) in a creative synthesis. In Otto's words, '. . . the numinous depth of the eternal One in and behind all things (including the perceiver) calls to the numinous depth of the soul in its inmost being' (p. 275).

Having indicated that the mystical experience may be conceptualized in trans-theistic and non-theistic terms, as well as theistic terms, I shall now advert to the question of the relationship between mystical and numinous experience. I shall try to show that there is a significant correlation between the types of mystical experience outlined above and the analysis of the numinous experience as the apprehension of a *Mysterium, Tremendum et Fascinans*.

As we have already noted in an earlier chapter, Otto distinguishes between rational and non-rational elements in religion. The rational concepts of religion must be predicated of a non-rational or supra-rational subject. Now Otto argues that it is mysticism which pre-eminently emphasizes the non-rational aspect of religion:

Mysticism enters into the religious experience in the measure that religious feeling surpasses its rational content, that is . . . to the extent to which its hidden non-rational, numinous elements predominate and determine the emotional life. (Otto 1932:159; see also, idem, 1958:22, 85 n., 197)

In the light of this passage it is quite clear that there is a *prima-facie* case for the subsuming of the mystical experience within the general type of the numinous experience by Otto. This can be substantiated by further examination of Otto's analysis of the numinous experience.

As an essential preliminary to a further examination of *'Mysterium, Tremendum et Fascinans'*, we must note that the numinous experience may be said to have occurred where any *one* of these epithets can be applied to that which is apprehended; i.e., the various aspects of the numinous experience may occur either singly or in combination. For example, the aspect of *mysterium* may occur without the element of awefulness which is included under the *tremendum* aspect, and *vice versa*. Otto notes (1958:25) that

The elements of meaning implied in 'awefulness' and 'mysteriousness' are in themselves definitely different. The latter may so far preponderate in the religious consciousness, may stand out so vividly, that in comparison with it the former almost sinks out of sight; . . . Occasionally, on the other hand, the reverse happens, and the *tremendum* may in turn occupy the mind without the *mysterium*.

Thus, we need not expect Otto's analysis of the mystical experience to be integrally correlative with *all* the aspects of the numinous experience, nor aspects of each type of mystical experience to be equally correlative with *all* the aspects of the numinous experience. If it can be shown that the mystical experience may be correlated significantly with some of the numinous aspects, this will be sufficient evidence for the subsuming of mystical experience within the general category of numinous experience, or at least, as far as Otto is concerned.

The *tremendum* aspect of the numinous experience is divided by Otto into the three elements of awefulness, overpoweringness, and energy. In the higher religions, the element of awefulness appears as a feeling of personal nothingness and submergence before the awe-inspiring object which is so experienced. It is possible to relate this 'awefulness' element to Otto's analysis of the Mysticism of Unifying Vision since in the highest stage of that experience there is the recognition that only the *One* exists. Otto's remark (1958:17) that the feeling of personal nothingness before the *numen* is evoked by 'mystical awe' would certainly point in that direction. However, this remark is not sufficiently elucidated to sufficiently justify such a correlation.

The case is otherwise with respect to the element of overpoweringness (*majestas*). This element evokes in the recipient of the experience the consciousness of being dust and ashes. It is crucial to note that Otto is concerned to differentiate this feeling of overpoweringness from Friedrich Schleiermacher's (1948) 'feeling of absolute dependence'. Otto argues, quite correctly, that by this 'feeling of absolute dependence' Schleiermacher means the consciousness of being conditioned, of being a created being, and that this consciousness is related to the notion of a Creator-being. Otto points out that, for this reason, Schleiermacher develops the implications of this sense of createdness in his sections on Creation and Preservation in *The Christian Faith*. By contrast, Otto maintains that the feeling of overpoweringness is not that of createdness but rather the consciousness of *creaturehood*. Thus, he indicates that the conceptualization of the aspect of overpoweringness in terms of a causal relationship between Creator and created does not come to terms with the full import of this aspect. Rather, if reason attempts to analyse this aspect, it generates the notion of the non-reality of the self and the sole reality of the *numen*:

In the one case you have the fact of having been created; in the other, the status of the creature. And as soon as speculative thought has come to concern itself with this latter type of consciousness . . . we are introduced to a set of ideas quite different from those of creation or preservation. We come upon the ideas, first, of the annihilation of self, and then, as its complement, of the transcendent as the sole and entire reality. (Otto 1958:21)

In our analysis of the Mysticism of Unifying Vision, it was seen that Otto maintains that the second stage of this kind of mystical experience may be conceptualized in theistic terms, in terms of Creator and created. We saw also that Otto maintains that this second stage of conceptualization may be transcended by a third which may be conceptualized in terms of the One as the sole and entire reality. This mystical schema is significantly parallel to the schema outlined in the above discussion of the meaning of *majestas*. On the basis of this correlation, we may make two preliminary conclusions. Firstly, the mystical experience of Unifying Vision is subsumable under the *majestas* element of the numinous experience. And therefore secondly, the numinous experience may be conceptualized in theistic terms (God, Creator, Cause of the Universe, etc.) but such conceptualization may be transcended, and the *numen* described in trans-theistic terms (The Only Real, Brahman, the Godhead).

Turning to the element of Energy, this is most correlative to mysticism when combined with *majestas*. In this combination, there is the welling up of 'a force which is urgent, active, compelling, and alive'. This urgency, activity, and compellingness is a significant factor, according to Otto, in 'voluntaristic' mysticism. It is evidenced in such mysticism 'in that "consuming fire" of love whose burning strength the mystic can hardly bear' (1958:24). While the element of energy is not correlative with Otto's analysis of mysticism into its two prevailing types, its presence is nevertheless a major criterion for distinguishing the mysticism of Eckhart from that of Shankara. While the mysticism of the latter is centred upon the rigid and static 'Being' Brahman, the Godhead of Eckhart flows out of and returns to itself as 'both the principle and the conclusion of a mighty inward *movement*, of an eternal process of ever-flowing life' (Otto 1932:187). Otto remarks (ibid., p. 193),

Eckhart's conception of God is thoroughly voluntarist. His Esse is will as an eternally active and dynamic principle in contrast to a rigid and static Being.

The *mysterium* is designated the *stupendum* by Otto. The *numen* is a mystery which arouses stupor and amazement. As *mysterium*, the *numen* is wholly other, quite beyond the sphere of the usual, the intelligible. The wholly other aspect reaches its zenith in mysticism:

Mysticism continues to its extreme point this contrasting of the numinous object (the *numen*), as the 'wholly other', with ordinary experience. (Otto 1958:29)

According to Otto, the extreme point of this contrasting of the *numen* and ordinary experience is reached when the *numen* is designated as 'that which is nothing' (nothingness, *shūnya*, *shūnyatā*), as that about which nothing can be said or thought. He writes (ibid.),

Not content with contrasting it with all that is of nature or this world, mysticism concludes by contrasting it with Being itself and all that 'is', and finally actually calls it 'that which is nothing'.

The wholly other aspect of the *numen* correlates with our earlier analysis of mysticism in two ways. Firstly, it is the wholly other aspect of the *numen* which generates the ascending stages of the Mysticism of Unifying Vision. That is, it is the quest to indicate the qualitative otherness of the apprehended *numen* which evokes its eventual expression as the Only Real. From the above passage, it would also appear that even this expression can be transcended by a complete denial of all predicates as applicable to the Real. Suffice it for us to note therefore, that the mystical schema of Unifying Vision as outlined earlier is part of a logical progression towards this ulimate stage of silence.

Secondly, the wholly other aspect of the *numen* may also be seen as correlative with that which lies at the basis of the individual. Otto maintains (1958:203) that what is true of the supreme, spiritual Being (the *numen* external to the self) is also true of the human soul or spirit:

In us, too, all that we call person and personal, indeed all that we can know or name in ourselves at all, is but one element in the whole. Beneath it lies, even in us, that 'wholly other', whose profundities, impenetrable to any concept, can yet be grasped in the numinous self-feeling by one who has experience of the deeper life.

The conceptualization of this 'numinous self' occurs most rigorously according to Otto in the doctrine of souls in Indian *Sānkhya*. Nevertheless, even this extreme conceptualization and systematization

. . . cannot entirely conceal the fact that 'Soul' or *Ātman* is *properly* the thing of marvel and stupefaction, quite undefinable, outsoaring all conceptions, 'wholly alien' to our understanding. (Ibid., p. 195)

In summary therefore, the Mysticism of Introspection is intimately connected with the *mysterium* aspect of the numinous experience since that which is apprehended in the introspective experience has an explicitly numinous flavouring.

Moreover, it is because of the numinousness both of the self and of that which lies beyond the self (the One, the Real, etc.) that there is the possibility of the intertwining of the two ways of mysticism. Thus,

For however different it may be, on the one hand the discovery of the miraculous depths of the soul and God indwelling in the heart of man, and on the other the depth of the world in unity and oneness: both are above all experiences of *wonder*. . . . To express it roughly: Brahman and ātman are both descended from a 'numinous sphere'. (Otto 1932:278–279)

With the *fascinans* element, there is also possible a transition to mysticism. At its highest point, the fascinating becomes the over-bounding, the exuberant. Thus, of the Buddhist experience of Nirvāna, Otto maintains (1958:39) that

It is only conceptually that 'Nirvana' is a negation; it is felt in consciousness as in the strongest degree positive; it exercises a 'fascination' by which its votaries are as much carried away as are the Hindu or the Christian by the corresponding objects of their worship.

The *fascinans* element in connection with mysticism may be spoken of as 'Bliss-unspeakable' (ibid., p. 39; these are not Otto's words, but were addressed to him by a Buddhist monk as a description of *Nirvāna*).

On the basis of the above exposition, we may generate the following further conclusions. Firstly, the mystical experiences of Unifying Vision and of Introspection both involve the *mysterium* aspect of the numinous experience and are thus subsumable within that experience. Secondly, the numinous experience may therefore be conceptualized in non-theistic terms, for example, soul, *ātman, purusha*, etc. Thirdly, some general aspects of mysticism are correlative with the aspect of urgency and the element of *fascinans*.

The implication of the conclusions generated in this chapter thus far are clear. Firstly, analysis of Otto's exposition of the numinous experience will need to take into account the much wider ramifications of the numinous experience as presented above. Secondly, either defence of or criticism of Otto needs to be based upon the fundamental premiss of interpretation established in this chapter — that the numinous experience may be conceptualized in theistic, trans-theistic, and non-theistic terms. Thirdly, when we take into consideration both the examination of Otto in Chapter two, and our analysis in this chapter, then we may say that for Otto, there is one general kind of religious experience, the numinous experience, and under this umbrella may be sheltered (at least) three different varieties of this experience — theistic experience, introvertive mystical experience, and extrovertive mystical experience. Nevertheless, and fourthly, we have again put forward reasons for expressing doubt as to the role of extrovertive experience in the establishing of or reinforcing of religious doctrines.

It is beyond doubt that phenomenologically, the awe-inspiring theistic experiences of Isaiah, Arjuna, and Mohammed are quite distinct from the mystical experiences of introvertive unity in Eckhart and Shankara. Thus, while we have shown that Smart's exegesis of Otto is incorrect, for Otto does not ignore mystical experience in his analysis of numinous experience, the question nonetheless remains why Otto should have placed such phenomenologically disparate varieties of religious experience under the one broad category of the numinous. And further, why does Otto, in spite of his own predilection for Christianity, seem to make mystical experience the experience most correlative to the core of religion, *viz.* the non-rational apprehension of a *Mysterium, Tremendum et Fascinans*? In what follows, I shall attempt to indicate that the answer to both these questions lies in

Otto's adoption of the Kantianism of Jakob Fries as the philosophical substructure of his phenomenological enquiry. In particular, I shall outline Otto's notion of the Holy as an *a priori* category and the relationship between numinous experience and the Friesian concept of *Ahnung (Ahndung)*.[5]

Fries's philosophy stands firmly in the Kantian tradition and yet modifies the Kantian theories considerably. According to Kant, experience is the product of formal elements contributed by the mind itself and the experience of the senses which has for us the form of the pure intuitions, space and time. The basic formal elements of the mind, the categories, are our ways of bringing the diverse data of experience into a unity of understanding. The original unity, and its articulation in the categories does not derive from understanding or intellect. Rather, it is completely *a priori*. Its application to human experience is universal and necessary. Nevertheless, there is quite clearly a strain of subjectivism in Kant. Otto expresses it in this way (1931:18):

> The discovery of this 'a priori' in general was the great task of the Kantian Criticism of Reason. But, in establishing the a priori types of knowledge, Kant had at the same time made the perilous affirmation that their validity was merely subjective and that whatever was known through them was 'ideal'.

According to Otto, Fries improved upon the philosophy of Kant in two ways. Firstly, Otto believes that Fries has shown that there *is* immediate knowledge of reality, independent of perception, and produced by pure reason. The content of this knowledge is the notion of the objective synthetic unity of all the manifold given in sense. Otto writes (1931:49, see also p. 52),

> He [Fries] proves that all nature-concepts are merely the various forms of one fundamental idea of the reasoning mind — the idea of universal unity and necessity; or, differently expressed, that they are single and individual determinations of the fundamental knowledge about the necessity and unity of everything that *is*, in general, which rests on the foundation of every single Reason as something most immediate and most profound.

Secondly, Otto claims that Fries has improved upon Kant by means of his notion of *Ahnung*. David Bastow (1976) points out that the judgements of sense experience do not directly reveal the relation between those objects the knowledge of which is basic to sense perception, and the whole of absolute reality. To put it crudely, sense experience does not and cannot reveal the relation of the fundamental knowledge of unity to knowledge of multiplicity. Nevertheless, Fries asserts that this relationship can be *felt*, can be *intimated*, and this feeling or intimation (*Ahnung*) is characterized as aesthetic judgement. This feeling leads, for anyone who has it, to a realization that the Ideas are not merely formal and empty but have content, and therefore can be said to be valid:

The aesthetic idea is a form of the *unity* of the multiplex, a form that cannot be expressed. In our conceptions of Nature and in the ideas we attain real knowledge of Unity (and of Necessity) in things. In the aesthetic judgement the perception of the multiplex thus comes in an undefined way under the power of the concepts of Nature and of the Ideas. That is to say, in an undefined, obscure manner, by the way of 'Ahnung' I gain real knowledge of the universe in a quite particular way, following the supreme laws of its unity and necessity, which are clearly presented in conceptual form in the Categories as a whole. . . . In aesthetic ideas I gain an obscure comprehension of the unity and connection of true reality in the world of appearance, of this reality in its essential nature. (Otto 1931:141)[6]

Both of these modifications of Kant by Fries are of importance for Otto's theory of religion, and therefore, for our understanding of Otto. With respect to the first, it enabled Otto to utilize a philosophical theory to rescue religion from its reduction to metaphysics in the case of the pre-Kantian rationalists, and to ethics in the case of Kant. Moreover, Fries's 'objectivizing' of the Kantian framework enabled Otto to both establish religion as having its roots in a distinct kind of experience with its own *a priori* categories, and to argue that such experience has objective validity (1931:223). In another context, speaking of 'intuitions' and 'feelings' in Schleiermacher, Otto writes (1958:147),

. . . they must certainly be termed *cognitions*, modes of *knowing*, though, of course, not the product of reflection, but the intuitive outcome of feeling. Their import is the glimpse of an Eternal, in and beyond the temporal and penetrating it, the apprehension of a ground and meaning of things in and beyond the empirical and transcending it.[7]

The above passages also give us some indications of Otto's use of the notion of *Ahnung*. Specifically, *Ahnung* is equivalent to the numinous experience. The following passage leaves us in no doubt whatsoever. Summarizing Fries's philosophy, Otto says (1931:223),

. . . in all these respects this philosophy reveals the disposition to religion in the spirit of man in general, the hidden source of all its manifestations in history, the ground for its claim to be true, to be indeed the supreme and ultimate Truth.

We began this section by asking why Otto placed such phenomenologically disparate varieties of religious experience under the one broad category of numinous experience. We may now broach an answer to this question. In the final chapter of his *The Philosophy of Religion*, Otto describes two starting points to the true Science of Religion. The first of these is the 'empirico-inductive' investigation of religions which will secure a proper conception of the real nature of religion. The focal point of this study will be religious experience. The other starting point follows the work of the *Critique of Reason* as a whole with a view to generating a metaphysic of religion. Otto claims that these two paths, although at first different, must ultimately meet. Bastow (1976:169) offers the following appropriate comment:

But how can Otto claim to know that the paths will meet? My suggestion is that this is only because he builds assumptions taken from his philosophical position into his supposedly empirico-inductive investigation, i.e. he *assumes* a phenomenological unity based on religious experience, and considers that he merely has to find out its nature. In summary, to share Otto's confidence about the fundamental unity of all religious experience and hence basically of all religion, we must first adopt his Friesian metaphysic, and second provide the argument Otto omits, to show the paths must meet.

By way of summary, therefore, we may note that it is the adoption by Otto of the Friesian notion of *Ahnung* and the development of the notion of the *a priori* category of the Holy which both militate against Otto taking note of the phenomenological disparities we have been referring to, and persuade him to place both theistic and mystical experience within the broad category of the numinous experience.

A further point is of some value. Bastow wishes to enquire about the relation between Fries's *Ahnung* and Otto's experience of the numinous. As he points out, the general description of *Ahnung* is of an aesthetic experience in which the world is seen as one and as necessary. He continues (1976:170),

This realization of the unity of transcendental apperception as a whole would be quite distinct from experience of a numen, separated by an infinite and aweful gulf from the earthly being who experiences him.

In so far as *Ahnung* is compared to numinous experience when conceptualized in theistic terms, Bastow's point is a valid one. Nevertheless, as we have seen in an earlier part of this chapter, it need not be so conceptualized. For, mystical expressions are conceptualizations of the numinous experience, and, in so far as these express a fundamental unity behind the multiplicity of the phenomenal world, there is a comparability between *Ahnung* and the numinous experience to the extent to which the hidden non-rational elements of numinous experience predominate. To put it simply, mystical experience and *Ahnung* do seem similar. There is a hint to this effect in a description of the experience of *Ahnung* by Otto (1931:93, my italics):

It is in the truest sense a Platonic *anamnesis* of the Idea, and through it alone is conceivable the unspeakable profundity, the mighty rapture, the spell of mystery that plays around this experience. . . . Here 'mystery in religion' comes into play. Religion itself is an experience of mystery; not the sort of mystery which would only exist for the uninitiated, which would be solved for the adept, but the sensible mystery of all existence in Time as a whole — eternal reality breaking through the veil of temporal existence, to the unlocked heart. Here is the truth which underlies all 'mystic' excess and imagination; *here is the seat of the mystic element in all religion.*

There are then intimations of the proposed connection of mystical experience and *Ahnung* in the above passage. It would of course be most useful if the connection could be made with reference to Otto's *Mysticism East and West*. In fact, Otto develops, but unfortunately only briefly, the relationship between Friesian philosophy and introvertive and extrovertive mystical experience. He remarks that in so far as for Kant all perceptions of unity, meaning, and value rise from a depth of mind beneath the level of senses and understanding, he too knows the 'ground of the soul'. He goes on to maintain that Fries has developed this further in his doctrine of Transcendental Apperception:

This transcendental apperception is formed through the unifying functions of 'formal' apperception, and this in turn is a fundamental and primordial knowledge of eternal unity and fulfilment. This basic cognition of Fries' doctrine could not be otherwise or better described than by the mystical intuition of Eckhart, which is also not an individual act of empirical consciousness, but a fundamental element of the soul itself, independent of all here and now, and only in individual moments breaking forth out of its depth to actualize itself in empirical consciousness. (1932:266)

In another context, Otto argues that where the capacity to perceive the self through the Mysticism of Introspection is awakened, so also the capacity to perceive the unity behind the multiplicity of phenomena is awakened. He gives the following Friesian interpretation of this (1932:281):

In the language of secular speech we should have to say: 'Knowledge of the (mystical) unity of the universe and of my own unity with it is Knowledge a priori'. The senses provide the raw material for this. But what this 'is', what it 'is' in truth, wherein lies its depth, meaning and essence, the senses do not reveal. This is also discovered immediately by the soul 'through itself', and that means that the soul finds it 'indwelling' in itself.

Hopefully, sufficient has been said to indicate the close correlation between *Ahnung* and Otto's account of mystical experience. The implications of this are deserving of a little more expansion. Firstly, this, when taken together with the connection of the numinous experience and *Ahnung*, reinforces considerably our earlier analysis of the relation of mystical and numinous experience. There is however a more far-reaching implication. It would be unwise of me, both in the light of the brevity of the foregoing discussion and in the light of Otto's style which is most often evocative rather than analytic, to make too strong an assertion. Nevertheless, our discussion would suggest that the limiting form of the non-rational component of religious experience is mystical experience, and therefore, that, to the extent that philosophical truth is identified with religious truth, those religious experiences which are conceptualized in theistic terms are less 'in touch with absolute reality' than those experiences conceptualized in mystical modes of expression. This is not to suggest that this is Otto's intended position. For, at another level, the most true religion for Otto is that which is the furthest developed in the translation of the non-rational component of religion into metaphysical and moral conceptual structures and this religion is, without doubt for Otto, Christianity (1958:1[8]). Nevertheless, I would suggest that something of this sort is implied by both the philosophical substructure and the phenomenological analysis of mystical experience offered by Otto. Thus, there is, at the very least, a possible incompatibility between the implications of his phenomenological-philosophical approach to religious truth and his own predilection to delineate Christianity as the highest religion by a different criterion of religious truth. (For a recent Kantian approach to religious experience which appears to get into difficulties similar to Otto's, see Hick 1977b.) And further, committed as it appears to be to the idea that religious truth relates both to religion in its most non-rational manifestation, i.e. numinous experience, and religion in its most rational manifestation, i.e. Christianity, this possible incompatibility within Otto's theory of religion does not appear easy of resolution.

6

A Comparative Analysis

In this study we have been concerned with the relationship between religious experience — especially mystical experience and, to a lesser extent, theistic experience — and doctrinal formulation in religion. Specifically, we have examined the relationship between these, by reference to the models of mystical experience proposed by S. Radhakrishnan, R. C. Zaehner, N. Smart, W. T. Stace, and Rudolf Otto. At this juncture, it is fruitful to look at these models to see how they relate to each other and to attempt to draw together the results of our study thus far.

It is apparent from our study that all those with whom we have dealt recognize that mystical experience must be taken into account as a major factor in religious formulations. For Radhakrishnan, spiritual or religious experience *is* mystical experience and it is on the basis of this presupposition that the philosophy of tolerance and the thesis of the unity of all religions is developed. On the other hand, Zaehner wishes to argue that such a philosophy of tolerance is not acceptable. This is for the reason that, according to him, there are different varieties of mystical experience which such a philosophy does not take into account. Thus, he argues that there is not only a clear distinction between mystical experience with the eyes open — panenhenic experience — and mystical experience with the eyes closed, but that there are two different varieties of non-sensory mystical experience, the monistic and the theistic mystical, of which the latter is the higher form. In the latter part of Chapter one, the thesis of the unity of all religions was also criticized on the grounds that, on the one hand, it unjustifiably viewed one kind of religious experience as normative thereby ignoring other possible forms of religious experience and, on the other hand, that it assumed that 'higher truth' was expressed in a particular mainstream tradition of Hinduism, namely, that in which the essence of the self is identical with the Godhead.

In contrast to Zaehner, however, we have noted that Smart, Stace, and Otto all argue that there is only one form of interior mystical experience. I have argued that Zaehner's claim for theistic mystical experience was not validated by his analysis, and therefore also, that his claim that theistic mystical experience was a higher form of mystical experience, was not acceptable. Nevertheless, this did not entail our accepting the thesis of Smart, Stace, and Otto that there is a phenomenological unity of interior mystical experience. Rather, the possibility that there are for example phenomenologically theistic mystical experiences was left quite open. We shall need to consider this possibility much more fully in a subsequent chapter.

We may further note that only two of the writers examined saw the necessity of including theistic experience in their analysis, namely, Smart and Otto. Such an omission by Radhakrishnan and Zaehner must count against the comprehensiveness of their accounts. In the case of Stace, we noted that the exclusion of such experience probably derived from his philosophical critique of the possibility of such experience; that is to say, according to him the naturalistic principle forbids us to believe that there ever occur interruptions in the normal course of events by a supernatural being. If Stace's exclusion of theistic experience arises from such a principle, and it most probably does, then this does not justify the exclusion of theistic experience from consideration. For, even if it is the case that the naturalistic principle is perfectly valid, theistic experiences nevertheless still do occur. What the naturalistic principle does forbid is not the recognition that theistic experiences play an important role in doctrinal formulations, but rather, the claim that such experiences occur as the result of the intervention of a supernatural being. And this is perhaps another example of the confusion of phenomenology and philosophy in Stace's work.

Smart, as we have seen, includes theistic experience (somewhat unfortunately called 'numinous experience' by him) in his analysis. According to him, expressions which appear to be derived from theistic mystical experience are to be distinguished from non-theistic mystical expressions by the ramifying presence of doctrines derived from theistic experience. Furthermore, the differences between, for example, Advaita Vedānta and the mystical expression of St. Teresa of Avila are to be explained by different priority decisions made within different traditions between the numinous strand and the mystical strand. In essence therefore, for Smart, the religious traditions may be seen as consisting of the numinous or mystical strands, or the subtle interweaving of the two.

Similarly, for Rudolf Otto, theistic experience is taken into account. For Otto however, in contrast to Smart, both theistic and mystical experience are placed under the one category of the numinous. I have argued that this classification is not warranted because of the phenomenological disparity of mystical and theistic experience, and have indicated that it arises, not from phenomenological analysis, but rather from philosophical presuppositions derived from the Kantian metaphysics of Jakob Fries.

With reference to extrovertive mystical experience, we have seen that Zaehner, Stace, and Otto all argue that its occurrence must be taken into account in an analysis of mystical expressions. Furthermore, we criticized Smart for his exclusion of such experience on the basis that his grounds for such exclusion were unjustified. Nevertheless, it has been indicated at various points in this study that while panenhenic or extrovertive modes of expression may be discerned in mystical texts, these are not to be taken as expressive of a unique kind of experience. Rather, in the absence of any autobiographical evidence to the contrary, such modes of expression ought to be seen as the expression of reflection upon the world subsequent to a unitive or introvertive experience and prevalent within those traditions which have an incipient thrust towards a philosophical absolutism. To this extent, Smart's exclusion of such extrovertive experience is vindicated, albeit on quite different grounds.

We may summarize the similarities and differences between these writers in the following series of propositions:
(1) For Radhakrishnan, there is one kind of religious experience, *viz.* the mystical;

(2) for Zaehner, there are three varieties of mystical experience — the panenhenic, the monistic, and the theistic;

(3) for Smart, there are two main varieties of religious experience — the numinous (theistic) and the mystical;

(4) for Stace, mystical experience admits of two varieties — the extrovertive and the introvertive;

(5) for Otto, both theistic experience and two varieties of mystical experience (the Inward Way and the Outward Way) are classified under the general category of numinous experience.

Within the context of their descriptions and classifications of religious experience — and mystical experience in particular — each of the theories we have examined has proposed a solution to the conflicting truth claims problem. According to Radhakrishnan, there is an underlying core of truth standing over against or lying behind the religious traditions which only partially enshrine it. In criticism of Radhakrishnan, it was argued that such a claim makes a covert assumption that religious truth is ultimately dependent upon mystical experience. To the extent that this assumption is a covert one and is not argued for, Radhakrishnan has adopted a normative stance which cannot be accepted.

For Ninian Smart, the most valid form of doctrinal framework is that which combines both the numinous and mystical strands with the former predominant. Against Smart, it was argued that, in the final analysis, he is caught in a conceptual bind since his conceptual framework entails both that the truth of any interpretation of religious experience depends in large measure on factors external to the experience, and also that if we are to find religious truth, we should look to religious experience.

It may also be noted at this point that we suggested that Rudolf Otto was in somewhat the same dilemma. Otto was committed on the one hand to arguing that truth in religion is closely related to the non-rational factors therein and these factors are particularly prevalent in mysticism. On the other hand, his own penchant for Christianity orientated him towards a theory of religious truth which deemed the most true religion to be that religion which is the most highly developed morally and theologically, namely, Christianity.

Zaehner, albeit on quite different grounds, is in agreement with Smart that candidacy for religious truth is most likely to be found in systems of theistic mysticism. Our criticism of Zaehner depended on the argument that his textual examples were not persuasive and that his criteria for the superiority of theistic mysticism were most probably normative ones.

Finally, in the case of Stace, it was argued that there was a large measure of incompatibility between his phenomenological analysis and his conceptual claims concerning the truth of pantheistic interpretations of mystical experience. It was shown that pantheistic interpretations could not be said to be actual reflections of the mystical experience and that such pantheistic examples as were cited by Stace were better explained by alternative means.

To summarize: Although all of the models, to varying degrees of validity, demonstrate the nexus between mystical (and theistic) experience and doctrinal formulations, the resolution of the problem of conflicting truth claims between different religious traditions has not been accomplished by any of the models heretofore examined.

In the next chapter, it will be argued that this conceptual impasse is due in the main to the respective notions of the relationship between mystical experience and its interpretation. By an analysis of various theses of the relationship between experience and interpretation we shall hope, as far as is possible, to delineate in some detail the nature of and grounds of this impasse.

PART TWO

Towards a Conceptual Framework
for the Study of Mysticism

7

Mystical Experience and its Interpretation:
An Analysis of Possible Models

In the preceding chapters of this study, we have been concerned with a number of attempts to resolve the problem of conflicting religious truth claims within the context of the description and classification of (in particular) mystical experience. And we have seen how the nature and validity of these resolutions abuts on the question of the nature and validity of the respective descriptions and classifications of mystical experience. It is clear also from the comparative analysis in the previous chapter that there are disagreements not only in the proffered resolutions of the problem of conflicting religious truth claims, but also in the analyses of mystical experience we have examined.

It is my intention in the next several chapters to explore the nature and grounds of these latter disagreements. More specifically, I hope to demonstrate that these and other various accounts of the nature of mystical experience are the result of differing methodological assumptions about the relationship between mystical experience and its interpretation; and therefore, I hope to show that the validity of any account of mystical experience is dependent, and crucially so, on the cogency of these methodological assumptions.

Our task is, in consequence, not primarily an empirical one. Nothing is to be gained by the accumulation of more data. On the contrary, it is the abundance of data, and its multifarious nature, which generates the essential interpretative question with which we have to deal, namely, that of the relationship between religious doctrines and the mystical experience or experiences to which they may refer.

We shall proceed initially by critically analysing a number of possible models of the relationship between mystical experience and its interpretation and, in the light of this, aim to develop a more cogent one. As a consequence of the model thus developed it will be possible to propose a number of hypotheses on the nature of mystical experience and to suggest a number of procedures pertinent to the investigation of them.

The first task in this chapter is then to outline five possible models of the relationship between mystical experience and its interpretation. These are as follows:

(M1) All mystical experience is the same. There is a unanimity about mystical utterance which points towards the unanimity of mystical experience.

(M2) All mystical experience is the same but the various interpretations of the experience depend on the religious and/or philosophical framework of the mystic.

(M3) There is a small number of types of mystical experience which cut across cultural barriers.

(M4) There are as many different types of mystical experience as there are paradigmatic expressions of them.

(M5) There are as many different types of mystical experience as there are incorporated interpretations of them.

Before proceeding to a consideration of the first four of these in this chapter, it is necessary to point out that the boundaries between these models are to some extent fluid, as is perhaps only to be expected in a typology of this sort. Nevertheless, it is to be hoped that the models outlined above will be sufficiently useful to delineate the data and to enable our discussion to bear some fruit. Further, we ought to note that, within any discussion of mysticism, these models may operate at a number of levels. That is to say, while some accounts of mysticism openly declare their preference for one or other of these models, others imply such a preference, others entail it, and so on. We need therefore, in a number of cases, to tease out the model which is operative.

It can be noted too that the problem is here ignored, there avoided. Thus, for example, Sidney Spencer in his *Mysticism in World Religion* (1971) fails to advert to it at all, preferring rather to give an account of the varieties of mystical interpretations. And Geoffrey Parrinder (1976:11–16), while clearly aware of the problem, nonetheless in effect avoids dealing with it. Though he appears sympathetic to Zaehner's analysis, his sights are set firmly on the various interpretations, and not on the experiences to which they are or may be related. Be that as it may, we shall now examine the first of the above-mentioned models, namely, that the unanimity of mystical utterances points toward the unanimity of mystical experience.

In his book, *The Varieties of Religious Experience* (1961:329), William James makes the following remark:

In Hinduism, in Neoplatonism, in Sufism, in Christian mysticism, in Whitmanism, we find the same recurring note, so that there is about mystical utterances an eternal unanimity which ought to make a critic stop and think, and which brings it about that the mystical classics have, as has been said, neither birthday nor native land.

According to James, this recurring note is that of the overcoming of all barriers between the individual and the Absolute. On the basis of such purported unanimity in mystical utterance, James makes the following claim with regard to the nature of mystical experience (ibid.):

In mystic states we both become one with the Absolute and we become aware of our oneness. This is the everlasting and triumphant mystical tradition, hardly altered by differences of clime or creed.

Thus, in the light of the purported unanimity of mystical expression, James implies that there is but one kind of mystical experience.

A similar line of argument may be found in F. C. Happold's influential study and anthology *Mysticism* (1970). In a number of passages, the unanimity of mystical experience is entailed by the assertion of the unanimity of mystical expressions. He writes, for example (1970:20),

Not only have mystics been found in all ages, in all parts of the world and in all religious systems, but also mysticism has manifested itself in similar or identical forms wherever the mystical consciousness has been present. Because of this it has sometimes been called the Perennial Philosophy.

But Happold also exhibits the kind of theoretical confusion it is our concern to clarify. For he also wants to suggest that mystical experience can be divided into two types, the *mysticism of love and union*, and the *mysticism of knowledge and understanding* (ibid., p. 40). Here, it is clear that Happold is drawing on Zaehner's analysis. He goes on to talk about three aspects of mysticism, namely, nature mysticism, soul mysticism, and God mysticism. And thereby he signals an implicit commitment also to model three, the view that there is a small number of types of mystical experience which cut across cultural boundaries.

Commitment to model one is also implied in John Blofeld's account of Taoist mysticism. An assertion of the unanimity of mystical utterance is the ground for an argument towards the validity of mystical experience:

Confirmation of the genuineness of *the mystical* experience is to be found in the high degree of unanimity observable in the attempts to describe its nature. . . . If, as the cynics would have it, *the mystical* experience is sheer illusion, the stuff of dreams, it is strange that men and women belonging to widely different environments have, throughout the centuries, suffered the same delusions and dreamed the same dreams. (Blofeld 1970:25–26, my italics)

This first model is often present too in studies of mysticism which concentrate on one particular mystical tradition rather than proceeding from a comparative stance. Dom Cuthbert Butler (1967) in his classic study of Western mysticism finds a theological problem in what he sees as the unanimity of mystical utterances (1967:240):

But the experiences of all the mystics, non-Christian as well as Christian, are couched in the same language; all make, in one way or another, the same claim of entering into immediate relation and contact with the Divinity or with Ultimate Reality. The resemblance, the identity, of the descriptions are unmistakable for any one who will read the experiences on the one side and the other . . . Non-Catholic writers assume and assert the full identity of all such higher experiences, Catholic, Protestant, Mohammedan, Hindu. Has Catholic theology a place for fully supernatural religious mystical experiences outside of Catholic Christianity?

Similarly, W. R. Inge in his *Mysticism in Religion* (1969) finds unanimity in mystical utterance as reflective of a unanimity of mystical experience. On the basis of the harmony between a variety of definitions of Christian mystical experience, he concludes (p. 32), 'We shall find that this harmony is found, to a very remarkable extent, among mystics of all times, of all countries, and of all religions'. And finally, model one is implicit in J. B. Collins's *Christian Mysticism in the Elizabethan Age* (1971). Although this volume concentrates exclusively on Western mysticism, Collins nonetheless begins by asserting that 'The writings of the mystics, irrespective of time or country, show forth a number of common features' (1971:1), namely, an attempt to arrive at communion or union with an Absolute and final Reality.

Sufficient has been said to indicate the broad nature of the claim that there is a unanimity in utterance which indicates a unanimity of experience. And we can therefore begin a critique of it. The first point which needs to be made is simply this: In so far as we are referring to descriptions of that which is apparently encountered in mystical experience, rather than to general characteristics of the experience itself, then the claim that there is a unanimity in mystical utterance is false. It is true that the overall theme of a number of mystical traditions in Hinduism, Sūfism, and Christian mysticism is that of the nature of and quest for an Absolute or Ultimate Reality. But sufficient has been said already in this study to indicate that there are a number of mystic traditions — Theravāda Buddhism, Sānkhya-Yoga, Rāmānuja's Vishishtadvaita Vedānta — which express the mystical experience in quite different terms. Furthermore, as we have earlier noted, in the case of Mahāyāna Buddhism, there is a rejection of all views as to the nature of the ultimate 'realness' of things.

To be sure, the defenders of such an approach could argue that the above-mentioned exceptions are not exceptions by virtue of the fact that they do not include mystical utterances within their doctrines, texts, etc. A defence of this sort however, is bought at the expense of a vicious circularity. In a review of W. T. Stace's *Mysticism and Philosophy*, W. E. Kennick writes (1962:387),

Stace is impressed by the fact that mystics everywhere describe their experiences in similar ways; but this is surely not an occasion for surprise, since one recognises a man as a mystic largely by what he says. To be surprised at this fact is like being surprised at the fact that zebras have stripes.

It can therefore be seen that an arbitrary selection of mystics, for example, those who operate in traditions with a thrust towards absolutism, which is in effect what James, Happold, Butler, etc. do, effectively rules out our regarding the unanimity of mystical utterance as in any sense evidence for the unanimity of mystical experience.

In an article entitled 'Agreement Among Mystics', Galen Pletcher (1972) attempts to avoid the above-mentioned circularity. He agrees that if we determine who mystics are by examining the propositions the mystics maintain then we are involved in circularity. Nevertheless, he wishes to argue that there is an alternative means for determining who is to count as a mystic. This alternative means is the examination, not of the propositions maintained on the basis of the experience, but rather of the qualities or characteristics of the mystical experience. Thus, he claims, quite rightly I believe, that 'this procedure is not circular, because characteristics of the experience are used to select mystics, while their conclusions based on the experience are what is to be established by the argument from agreement' (1972:8).

In order to validate his point, Pletcher offers three lists of characteristics of mystical experience derived from James, Stace, and D. T. Suzuki. We shall now consider whether such lists of characteristics are sufficient to determine who shall count as a mystic.

The four characteristics of mystical experience determined by James (1961:299–300) are these:
(1) Ineffability;
(2) noetic quality;

(3) transiency;
(4) passivity.

Without labouring the point, let us consider the two qualities which James considers to be defining characteristics of mystical experience, namely, ineffability and noetic quality. With respect to the former of these, James gives the following account (ibid.):

The subject of it [mystical experience] immediately says that it defies expression, that no adequate report of its contents can be given in words. It follows from this that its quality must be directly experienced; it cannot be imparted or transferred to others.

James's definition of 'ineffability' is an accurate one, and while it is certainly the case that the mystical experience is often, though not always, delineated as such,[1] the notion of ineffability is not such as lends itself to the claim that different experiences have something in common in the sense that they are instances of the same or similar situations. In other words, the term 'ineffable' can fit incomparable experiences. Thus, Steven Katz writes (1978:48),

... an atheist can feel a sense of dread at the absurdity of the cosmos which he labels ineffable, while the theist can experience God in a way that he also insists is ineffable. Thus in *I and Thou*, Buber describes the dialogical encounter with God, the *Absolute Thou*, as ineffable, whose 'meaning itself cannot be transferred or expressed', while Kafka, whose brilliant and haunting tales also suggest the ineffability of existence intends no such encounter, nor reflects any faith in the existence of an *Absolute Thou*.

Turning to the characteristic of noeticity, we may venture a similar criticism. James defines this characteristic as follows (1961:300):

Although so similar to states of feeling, mystical states seem to those who experience them to be also states of knowledge. They are states of insight into depths of truth unplumbed by the discursive intellect.

Again, one would not wish to question the fact that mystics claim their experiences to be noetic. Nevertheless, the connection between mystical experience and noeticity is by no means an exclusive one. The point is made clearly by Katz (1978:49):

To argue, as James does, that because each such experience claims to give 'insight into depths of truth unplumbed by the discursive intellect' all the experiences are the same, fails to recognise both the variety of 'insights' one could have into the 'depths of truth' and the variety of 'truths' which can lurk in these depths waiting to be 'plumbed'. The varying claims made for such knowledge of the 'truth' is staggering, running from Pythagorean speculations to voodoo, animism, and totemism, to Madame Blavatsky's theosophy and Huxley's and Ramakrishna's *philosophia perennis*, to say nothing of the variety of more traditional religions.

Let us now advert to the lists of characteristics offered by Stace and Suzuki. According to Stace (1961:131–132), both extrovertive and introvertive experience share the following characteristics:
(1) Sense of objectivity or reality;
(2) feeling of blessedness, joy, happiness, satisfaction, etc.;
(3) feeling that what is apprehended is holy, sacred, or divine;
(4) paradoxicality;
(5) ineffability.
In addition to these five characteristics, we may recall that the extrovertive experience is differentiated from the introvertive by the former's entailing the proposition that 'all is One' and the latter's being the attainment of a unitary consciousness. The following characteristics are adduced by D. T. Suzuki (quoted in Stace 1961:20):
(1) Irrationality, inexplicability, incommunicability;
(2) intuitive insight;
(3) authoritativeness;
(4) affirmation (positive character);
(5) sense of the beyond;
(6) impersonal tone;
(7) feeling of exaltation;
(8) momentariness (coming of a sudden).
Turning first to W. T. Stace's list, Pletcher excludes from the list the unifying vision expressed by the formula 'all is One' on the grounds that such a criterion might pre-judge the propositions

a mystic might utter. We shall also exclude from the list the attainment of the Unitary Consciousness on the grounds, yet to be justified, that it invalidly excludes as mystical some experiences which do have some conceptual or symbolic content. This leaves us with characteristics one to five. Now there are a number of reasons why these characteristics are not definitive of mystical experience. Firstly, characteristics one, two, and three may be predicated of theistic experience just as appropriately as of mystical experience. Isaiah's experience of Yahweh in the Temple certainly evinces all these qualities as does also Arjuna's vision of Krishna in the *Bhagavad-Gītā*. Secondly, if these characteristics are taken as necessary ones, then characteristic three may well be taken as excluding certain apparent forms of mystical experience. Thus, for example, it is difficult to see Theravādin experience as fitting such a characteristic for it is difficult to assert that the experience is of the holy, the sacred, or the divine, or indeed that anything is apprehended at all. Thirdly, by virtue of the fact that two experiences are paradoxical, we are not thereby entitled to assume that they are the same experience. All we are entitled to assert is that two such experiences are similar to the extent that they are both claimed to be paradoxical. But we may make no further claim than this.

Without putting too fine a point on it, D. T. Suzuki's list comes under similar criticism. Characteristics two to eight and excluding six may all be said to correspond with the experience of Arjuna or Isaiah. While a tone of impersonality (characteristic six) is not characteristic of theistic experience, it may be said to be characteristic of certain experiences of the natural world. The classic example occurs in the writings of Pascal (*Pensées*, quoted in Zaehner 1972:16–17):

When I consider how short a time my life lasts — absorbed as it is in the eternity that precedes it and that which follows it — and how small is the space that I occupy or even that I can see, lost as I am in the infinite immensity of spaces which I do not know and which do not know me, I am appalled and wonder that I should be here rather than there. . . . The eternal silence of these infinite spaces appais me.

Moreover, while an impersonal tone is characteristic of much mystical expression, acceptance of this characteristic as a necessary one would necessitate the exclusion of mystical expressions of the love between God and the soul. If such expressions do reflect the phenomenological content of some mystical experience, then an impersonal tone cannot be accepted as a characteristic of mystical experience in general.

In summary therefore, Pletcher's suggestion that such characteristics may be utilized as a means of selecting mystics is not validated. This does not entail that such a set of characteristics does not exist. What it does mean, however, is that the most well known lists of mystical characteristics are not valid as such selection criteria since they both appear to exclude some obvious candidates for inclusion and include some just as obvious candidates for exclusion.

Nevertheless, let us assume for the moment that such a set of characteristics can be developed as the basis upon which to select mystics. And further, while recognizing the multifarious and diverse nature of mystical expressions, let us nevertheless consider the question whether propositions can be generated which are representative of the sort which mystics might maintain. If it can be shown that there are such propositions (or even one such proposition) of this sort, then this might provide at least some grounds for an assertion of the unanimity of mystical experience.

Consider the following proposition: 'There is an ultimate realness "beyond" the multiplicity of phenomena which cannot be apprehended by means of the normal modes of perception and conception' (Pletcher 1972:8 offers five other such propositions for consideration).

I believe that this proposition is broad enough to be a candidate for assent by all mystical traditions. To attempt to make such a proposition less broad by, for example, asserting that such 'ultimate realness' is that of a One behind the many or, of the ultimate unity of all multiplicity, would be to risk the rejection of the proposition by one or more traditions. To be sure, the proposition is so broad that it may include traditions which are not overtly mystical. This however is irrelevant to the matter in hand. It is only if this proposition can be made sense of that the question of its relationship to any other *particular forms* of religious expression becomes a pertinent one.

We may begin our consideration of this proposition by examining a comparison to such a proposition made by Terence Penelhum (1973). According to Penelhum, Plato, Aristotle, Spinoza, and Leibniz all created metaphysical systems which provide the person who has done the necessary intellectual and imaginative labour with a profound vision by means of which he may be enabled to understand the universe and the place of man in it. All these systems are distinguishable to this extent from the sceptical and anti-metaphysical philosophies of a Hume or a Wittgenstein:

It would not naturally occur to us to say, as a result of these similarities, that the doctrinal differences between them are merely superficial differences that mask a deeper identity of intent. For the similarities are the similarities that exist between those who accept a certain manner of proceeding in philosophy but get different results from it. . . . If you say that the differences between Spinoza and Leibniz are in some way not real differences, this is a way of rejecting both, not of accepting either. (Penelhum 1977:73)

The implications for our proposition are reasonably clear. Just as Plato, Aristotle, Spinoza, and Leibniz could agree that the 'ultimate realness' of the world cannot be apprehended apart from certain modes of metaphysical thought, so also would the mystical traditions assent to our proposition. However, assent to this proposition cannot disguise the real differences which appear were each mystical tradition to spell out what it meant by 'ultimate realness'. Steven Katz expresses this point most forcibly when he states (1978:51);

Henry Suso's 'intoxication with the immeasurable abundance of the Divine House . . . entirely lost in God [of Christianity]', the *Upanishad's* 'sat [what is] . . . is expressed in the word *satyam*, the Real. It comprises this whole universe: Thou art this whole universe', as well as the Buddhist's 'dimension of nothingness' (*ākincannāyatana*) all can be included under these broad phenomenological descriptions of 'Reality', yet . . . it is clear that Suso's Christian God is not equivalent to the Buddhist's 'nothingness', and that the experience of entering into the Divine House is not equivalent to losing oneself in Buddhist 'nothingness'. It becomes apparent on reflection that *different* metaphysical entities can be described by the same phrases if these phrases are *indefinite* enough.

By way of concluding this discussion of model one, we may note the following results. Firstly, in so far as we examine mystical utterances in their contexts, there is by no means an eternal unanimity. Secondly, any unanimity can only be bought at the expense of a vicious circularity. Thirdly, the attempt to avoid such circularity by an appeal to characteristics of the mystical experience as such is futile since the latter err by way of a far too broad inclusiveness or an unjustified exclusiveness. Fourthly, while propositions can be generated which would receive assent by mystical traditions, such propositions effectively mask deep underlying differences between mystical traditions. With respect to the nature of mystical experience, a number of conclusions have been reached. Firstly, we have seen that the argument from unanimity in mystical utterances to the unanimity of mystical experience is an unsound one. Such unanimity of mystical utterance cannot be demonstrated. Secondly, and perhaps more importantly, we have seen that it is difficult to define mystical experience in terms of lists of characteristics, and the attempt to determine the essence of mystical experience by paying attention to mystical propositions is fraught with difficulties. The necessity of seeking an alternative means to delineate mystical experience is therefore also foreshadowed in this discussion.

Let us now turn to consider model three, the view that there is a small number of types of mystical experience which cut across cultural barriers and which each receive their own characteristic modes of expression. During the course of this study, we have examined three instances of this model in the writings of Zaehner, Stace, and Otto. The significance of their accounts lies in the fact that their analyses of the mystical experience are adopted by a significant number of scholars working within different fields of mysticism. And, more importantly, their analyses are often accepted and applied in an uncritical way. Let me expand by considering firstly a number of accounts of the mysticism of Plotinus.

A. H. Armstrong (1969), for example, suggests that the varieties of mystical expression point towards the existence of varieties of mystical experience, and he appears therefore to be drawing on a model four approach. But his overall position is indicated when he appeals to Zaehner for support for his claim that Plotinus is essentially a theistic mystic. After a consideration of the relevant passages from the *Enneads*, he writes (1967:263),

> We seem bound, therefore, to draw the conclusion that the mysticism of Plotinus is not 'monistic' but 'theistic', using these rather vague terms in the reasonably precise sense given them by R. C. Zaehner ... It is, that is to say, a mysticism in which the soul seeks to attain a union with the Absolute of which the best earthly analogy is the union of lovers, not a mysticism in which the soul seeks to realize itself as the Absolute.

We can only read this passage as indicating a commitment to Zaehner's version of model three, that is, that the theistic mystical doctrines of Plotinus correspond to theistic mystical experiences. And Armstrong shows no awareness that alternative accounts of the relation of theistic mystical doctrines to mystical experience are possible. Something of the same sort must also be said of J. M. Rist's account (1967) of Plotinian mysticism. He wants to argue that a close analysis of the text can only lead to one conclusion, namely, that Plotinus was a theistic mystic. Using Zaehner's analysis as a guide, he concludes, 'Plotinus' mysticism can now be clearly seen to be of a theistic type, in Zaehner's sense of the word "theistic", and not monistic' (1967:228).

In contrast to both Armstrong and Rist, we may consider E. R. Dodds. Now Dodds prefers Stace's to Zaehner's account of the matter, and views Plotinus as a recipient of introvertive experiences. His reasons for this preference are a little difficult to discern. In part, it is because of the unanimity of mystical utterance; in part, because of his disapproval of the theological nuances in Zaehner's account of mystical experience; in part too, because his selection of texts from the *Enneads* allows him to place the emphasis elsewhere. The overall impression though, is that of an incipient and uncritical acceptance of the unity of introvertive mystical experience. It is very much a case of personal preference: '*In my view* it is recognisably the same psychological experience everywhere, however different the glosses that have been put upon it, however incompatible the theologies which it has been held to confirm' (Dodds 1965:86, my italics; see also, Wallis 1972:89, n.1).

A similarly uncritical acceptance of Stace's account may be found in R. E. L. Masters's and Jean Houston's attempt (1966:301–313) to examine the varieties of psychedelic experience. In their analysis of the relationship of drug and mystical experience, accounts of the nature of experiences caused by psychedelic drugs are correlated with Stace's account of mystical experience. In this case, the interpretative problem is doubly compounded. For not only is there the problem of the relationship of mystical experience to its interpretation, but also that of the connection of drug experience to accounts of it. And both relationships are ignored by Masters and Houston.

Finally, Raymond van Over, in the Introduction to his anthology of Chinese mysticism (1973) *merely asserts* his preference for Stace over Zaehner. After plotting the Chinese traditions on the grid of characteristics of mystical experience offered by Stace and Suzuki, he goes on to maintain that both extrovertive and introvertive experiences are to be found among the Chinese mystics. He concludes (1973:xxvi),

The variations found in the dogma of individual expressions of this experience do not change its fundamental nature. R. F. C. Zaehner, for instance, attempted a strictly Christian interpretation of this *unio mystica* and compares non-Christian mysticism unfavourably with the Christian experience. But arguing over the shape of a canister does not change its contents. . . . For whether it is called Godhead by Eckhart, or Brahman, Nirvana, Samadhi, Wu, Satori, Sunyata, does not alter the basic similarities or the experience's impact upon the human spirit and personality.

It is fruitful to review some of the conclusions reached in the earlier part of this volume in the light of this current discussion of model three. With reference to panenhenic or extrovertive modes of expression, where these occur in the context of religious systems, I have argued that these are not to be seen as reflections of a particular kind of religious experience. In other words, I have suggested that the leap from mode of expression to experience is unjustified. Rather, the claim has been made that such modes of expression are neither interpretations of extrovertive or of introvertive experience although they may be reinforced by experiences of the latter kind.

In the case of interior mystical experience, with reference to Stace's analysis, we have seen that the unanimity of such experience can only be gained by means of a crude notion of the relationship between experience and interpretation which both ignores contrary evidence supplied by Theravāda Buddhism and Sānkhya, and invalidly argues that any theistic mystical expression must be explained by the pressures of ecclesiastical orthodoxy.

That the interpretations of theistic mystics need to be taken seriously is certainly a point in favour of Zaehner. At this level, Zaehner is correct in his recognition of the need to recognize the diversity of mystical utterance. Nevertheless, I have argued that the interpretations of theistic mystical experience which Zaehner examines do not warrant his claim that they are interpretations of theistic mystical experience. Zaehner fails justifiably to bridge the gap between experience and interpretation. Furthermore, even if it were the case that the gap between theistic mystical experience and theistic mystical utterance were bridged, the question remains as to whether we would then need to postulate varieties of theistic mystical experience. The expression of the Mystic Kiss of Christ of St. Bernard is quite alien to St. Benedict's description of the Vision of God and also to St. Gregory's interpretation of it (see Butler 1967 : 86, 98). In fact, Zaehner's inability to take into account the diversity of mystical expression within his category of monistic mystical experience was also the basis of our earlier criticism of Zaehner. The differences in expression between Advaita Vedānta, Sānkhya, and Theravāda Buddhism were too great for them to be considered as reflections of merely *one* kind of experience.

In essence, therefore, while the recognition of the possibility of a larger variety of mystical experiences is present in Zaehner's writings as against those of Stace and Otto, he does not carry the logic of his methodology to its proper conclusion. That is to say, the methodology of determining the varieties of mystical experiences by an examination of post-experiential interpretation suggests the possibility of, not only a variety of mystical experiences within his monistic category, but also a variety of such experiences within his theistic category. In effect therefore, Zaehner's methodology does not commit him to model three but rather pushes him towards model four.

The view that there are as many varieties of mystical experience as there are paradigmatic expressions of it has not, to my knowledge, been offered as a thoroughgoing theory of the relationship between mystical experience and its interpretation. Nevertheless, it is implicit within a number of analyses of mystical experience to which we shall shortly refer.

For the purposes of our discussion, we may take the following definition of 'paradigmatic expression':

A paradigmatic expression of mystical experience is an expression which refers to the central focus (e.g. God, *Brahman*, *Nirvāna*), aim (e.g. attainment of union with God, attainment of *Kaivalya*), or nature (e.g. that it is objectless, non-dual, identity in difference), of the mystical experience.

In other words, model four is the view that there are as many types of mystical experience as there are variously expressed foci, aims, or descriptions of the nature of mystical experience. We can perceive model four in the analyses of G. J. Larson (1973:1–16)[2], M. Fakhry (1971:193–207) with respect to Indian and Islamic mysticism respectively, in Marghanita Laski's (1961) analysis of mystical states, and in an exposition of Walter Hilton's *The Ladder of Perfection* by H. P. Owen (1971:31–42).

According to Gerald Larson, the procedure by means of which the classification of the varieties of mystical experience is to be determined is examination of the various descriptions of *moksha* (release) within various Indian traditions:

In the complex religious traditions of India (Hindu, Jain, Buddhist, etc.) considered diachronically or synchronically, attempts to describe the mystical experience invariably involve a discussion of the search for and realization of 'emancipation', 'cessation', 'release', or 'freedom' — expressed most often by the terms *mokṣa, mukti, apavarga, kaivalya or nirvāṇa*. (Larson 1973:4)

In our terms, the paradigmatic expressions of the Indian mystical traditions are those which are intimately connected with the quest for liberation, more specifically, those which focus on the issues of *freedom-from* and *freedom-for*. From an analysis of four symbolic modes of expressing *moksha*, Larson proposes four varieties of Indian mystical experience — unitive, isolative, copulative, and nihilative. A brief résumé of these is in order.

Larson defines unitive mystical experience as '. . . the intuitive realization and understanding that any separation is somehow a threat or a terror, coupled with the realization that this threat can be overcome' (1973:6). From this perspective, the unitive mystical experience is freedom from all differentiation, all multiplicity, and all polarity, and freedom for the bliss of undifferentiated unity. Such experience finds its expression above all in the Upanishads (for example, the *Brihadāranyaka*, 2.4.11; the *Chāndogya*, 6.8.7; and the *Māndūkya*, 7) and in the later Vedāntic philosophical traditions, especially Advaita. In contrast to unitive experience, Larson argues that the isolative experience is determined by the necessity of overcoming the apparent ontological unity of the world. In Larson's terms, it is freedom from the undifferentiated unity of *purusha/prakriti* (in Sānkhya-Yoga) or *jīva/ajīva* (in Jainism) for the realization of the absolute distinction of *purusha* or *jīva* from *prakriti* or *ajīva*. This type of mystical experience involves '. . . a constant refusing to be reduced, on the one hand, to the oneness of nature and the world, and, on the other hand, to any kind of cosmic self or absolute' (Larson 1973:9).

Nihilative mysticism, represented pre-eminently by the Buddhist tradition, entails freedom from suffering, old age, and death, and freedom from a state of being beyond existence, self, Brahman, etc. Essentially, in this type of experience, nothingness or non-existence is the ground upon which the meaning of existence is revealed. By contrast, because of the affirmation of human existence in the world characteristic of the copulative experience, the copulative experience, embodied in the *Bhagavad-Gītā* (for example, 18.65), in the later traditions of theistic piety (Rāmānuja, Madhva, Caitanya), and in some Tantric traditions, means freedom from meaningless and undisciplined worldly existence, and freedom for responsible yet detached involvement in the world:

Man comes to realize that the fulfilment of himself comes from outside himself, and yet that very encounter from outside turns out to be experientially and theologically the manifestation of man's own innermost nature. The two entities or persons in the relationship, though separate and each fully real on one level, become one in the mystical experience. (Larson 1973:11, cf. Dasgupta 1927:124)

In the light of this brief exposition, it is apparent that Zaehner's category of theistic mystical experience is equivalent to Larson's category of copulative mystic experience and that Zaehner's monistic category is extended by Larson into the three varieties of unitive, nihilative, and isolative. In contrast to both Larson and Zaehner, Fakhry's utilization of model four generates, as we shall shortly see, a type of mystical experience not in evidence in either Zaehner's or Larson's categories.

As his criterion for discerning varieties of mysticism in Islam, Majid Fakhry draws a distinction between the mystical experience and the 'object' of such experience. It is his contention that the failure to discriminate between different possible objects of mystical experience has led to philosophical confusion. His main task therefore is to resolve the question whether the object sought in all forms of mysticism is the same one or different kinds of objects. By means of the above-mentioned criterion, Fakhry argues that there are three varieties of mysticism in Islam, namely, the philosophical, the visionary, and the unitary. He summarizes these in the following way:

The Divine (however it may be conceived) is the object of the second and the third variety, but not of the first. The apprehension or vision of this Divine is the purpose of the second, whereas union or identification with the Divine is the goal of the third; . . . A subordinate entity lying halfway between God and man is the object of the first, and theoretical communication or 'conjunction' with the object is its goal. (Fakhry 1971:194)

According to Fakhry, philosophical mysticism is associated with three principle figures — al-Fārābi, Ibn Sīnā, and Ibn Bājjah. Based on the Neo-platonism of Plotinus and Proclus,[3] reinforced by the Aristotelian notion of an unmoved Mover, and determined by the infinite difference between God and man necessitated by Qur'ānic teaching, the Muslim philosophical mystics forged into one identity the Aristotelian, Plotinian, and Qur'ānic deities. Such an identification led to the interposing of a series of ten intermediaries or emanations, between the world and the Godhead, the tenth of which dominates and superintends the world of generation and corruption and is the major focus of Muslim philosophical mysticism (see Fakhry 1971:197; also 1970:137–140, 174, for the process of emanation in al-Fārābi and Ibn Sīnā respectively). Of conjunction with this tenth emanation, the Active Intellect, Fakhry writes (1971:198; see also 1970:139),

The whole process of human cognition is described in terms of a progression from the lowest condition of potentiality to that of full actualization by means of 'conjunction' or contact (*ittisāl*) with this supermundane agency, which is the principal link between man and God. It is in this conjunction that the realization of man's intellectual potentialities, as well as his moral and spiritual vocation, consist.

Fakhry points out that there is a certain vacillation in the Muslim Neo-platonists as to the ultimacy of this state of conjunction. Both Ibn Sīnā and Ibn Bājjah suggest, on occasion, that conjunction may be transcended by union with God. Nevertheless, Fakhry indicates that the intellectual humanism characteristic of philosophical mysticism failed to appeal to the adepts of practical mysticism (the Sūfis) as well as to the theologians and the masses at large. For this reason, the visionary and unitary mystics, proclaiming as they did the apprehension of or union with the Deity, were of far more significance.

We need not devote much space to an exposition of the visionary and unitary mystical experiences for they are in effect Islamic instances of Zaehner's theistic category in the one case, and closely parallel to Larson's unitive experience in the other. Suffice it to say therefore, that the two principal representatives of visionary mysticism are al-Junayd and al-Ghazālī and the most typical representatives of unitary mysticism are al-Bastāmi and al-Hallāj. While in the case of the former pair, an ultimate distinction between man and God is maintained, for the latter pair, the complete identity of the self and God is asserted.

In summary, therefore, the paradigmatic expressions of philosophical mysticism, concerned as they are with a different focus to those expressions of unitary and visionary experience, are the means by which Fakhry determines that philosophical mystical experience is a separate variety within the Islamic tradition. By contrast, the determination that unitary and visionary paradigmatic expressions reflect different types of mystical experience arises from a distinction made, not between their respective objects, but rather between the variant expressions of the nature of such experiences.

Annemarie Schimmel in her *Mystical Dimensions of Islam* (1975:5–6) adopts a similar position to that of Fakhry. She too recognizes the modes of description referred to by Fakhry as the visionary and unitary under the titles of the mysticism of Infinity and the mysticism of Personality. And, like Fakhry, she suggests that there are two corresponding forms of experience. Thus, she implies her commitment to a model four approach.

In sum therefore, Larson, Fakhry, and Schimmel by implication, adopt the position that there are as many varieties of mystical experience as there are paradigmatic expressions of them. Now before proceeding to the accounts offered by Laski and Owen, it may be as well to outline a number of problems inherent in this model.

The major problem with this model is its central assumption. The problem lies in the fact that proponents of the model *assume* that paradigmatic expressions do reflect the actual phenomenology of the purported varieties of mystical experience. This assumption is not justified by the proponents of this model and indeed, it is not easy to see how paradigmatic expressions can be guaranteed to be 'verbal images' of mystical experiences. To this extent therefore, model four is circular for, in order to argue from a paradigmatic expression to a particular form of mystical experience, the question as to the relationship between paradigmatic expression and the phenomenological content of the mystical experience is begged.

Furthermore, to look upon the mystic as a mirror who accurately reflects the contents of his experience is to totally ignore the possible distortions of the experience in the mystic's interpretation. In short, model four does not take into account the mystic's own religious environment as a major factor in any expression of mystical experience.[4] Thus, model four, as also models one and three, fails to bridge the gap between experience and interpretation.

A further consideration is worthy of mention and this relates to the notion of the ineffability of the mystical experience. The question of the meaning of 'ineffability' with reference to mystical experience is a most bedevilling one and therefore a number of clarificatory points are necessary. Firstly, I do not wish to suggest that I support a position of radical ineffability which would assent to the proposition that mystics fail absolutely to communicate their experiences to non-mystics. There are a number of problems with such a position. Firstly, such a proposition is non-sensical. For if it is impossible for mystics to communicate their experiences to non-mystics, then there are no criteria by means of which we can determine who are mystics and who are not. The only possible commonality would reside in the fact that such experiences are radically ineffable. However, as we have seen earlier in this chapter, ineffability is not the exclusive prerogative of mystical experience and cannot be used as the sole determining criterion of such experience. Secondly, I believe that if any individual were to have an experience in which his personal ego was dissolved by melting into an ocean of undifferentiatedness, and which, furthermore, gave him a sense of utter peace and tranquillity, he could be fairly certain that he had experienced for himself that which is alluded to in a variety of mystical traditions. Thirdly, even where mystical experience is acknowledged as difficult of description this does not entail that it is impossible to communicate. P. G. Moore writes (1978:105),

. . . if mystics are using language at all responsibly then even what they say about the indescribable types or aspects of experience may at least serve to define them in relation to a known class of experiences. Thus when St. John of the Cross calls ineffable the experience of 'the touch of the substance of God in the substance of the soul', he is none the less communicating something of the experience by defining it in terms of the categories 'substance', 'touch', and so on.

Our second point of clarification arises from this. It is to the effect that it is necessary to distinguish three basic categories of mystical writings: (1) Autobiographical accounts of mystical experiences; (2) accounts, not necessarily autobiographical, in which mystical experience is described in generalized and abstract terms; (3) accounts referring to a mystical object or reality which do not refer, unless very obliquely, to mystical experience itself. P. G. Moore dubs these three categories of mystical writings first-order, second-order, and third-order categories respectively.[5] According to him, a large proportion of statements cited in support of radical ineffability come from the third-order category.[6] In contrast to third-order statements which are comprehensive and uncompromising in their reference, Moore maintains that first and second-order statements are usually partial and qualified in their reference. Thus, he quotes St. Teresa of Avila referring to one of the lower stages of the contemplative experience as 'easily understood by anyone to whom Our Lord has granted it, but anyone else cannot fail to need a great many words and comparisons' (Moore 1978:104). There is here no recognition of the impossibility of communicating to the non-mystic, but rather of the necessity to explain and illuminate as copiously as is possible. However, of a putatively higher stage of her experience, St. Teresa writes, 'I do not know if I have conveyed any impression of the nature of rapture: to give a full idea of it, as I have said, is impossible' (quoted in Moore 1978:104).

Moore argues that if, in some contexts, mystics say that an experience is describable, and in others, that it is beyond description, then this is not evidence of uncertainty or inconsistency but rather reflects the fact that a different stage or aspect of the experience is being referred to. (I find a similar example of such development in a passage from the autobiography of al-Ghazālī, see James 1961:317–318.)

What is the implication of the notion of 'ineffability' for our discussion? On the one hand, 'ineffability' does not necessitate the absolute impossibility of arguing from a paradigmatic expression of mystical experience to a claim about the nature of that experience. Nevertheless, our above discussion indicates that the possibility of a gap between the nature of mystical experience and its expression needs to be taken into account. Thus, if model four is to be justified, not only does it need to examine possible extra-experiential influences upon mystical interpretations (and this applies for all categories of mystical writings), but also it needs to examine the possibility that there is a 'looseness-of-fit' between mystical experience and its expression, and a complex interplay between the experience or the apprehended 'Reality' and the language, enmeshed as it is within our common stream of consciousness, which must perforce express that experience or that 'Reality'. Evelyn Underhill recognizes both of these necessities. She writes (1930:78–79), with reference to mystical symbolism,

The mind must employ some device of the kind if its transcendental perceptions — wholly unrelated as they are to the phenomena with which intellect is able to deal — are even to be grasped by the surface consciousness. . . . The nature of this [symbolic] garment will be largely conditioned by his [the mystic's] temperament . . . and also by his theological education and environment.

The problems of model four which we have just indicated would certainly appear to rule out of court the methodological procedure of Marghanita Laski in her book *Ecstasy* (1961). She is concerned primarily with what she calls spontaneous and momentary 'intensity ecstasy' rather than with 'withdrawal ecstasy', the trance-like nature of which arises from the pursuit of a contemplative method. As her main methodological tool she adopts a philological approach and bases her analysis upon the principles that 'some images are appropriate to one experience, some to another', and that 'common language derives from common experience rather than from deliberate or unconscious borrowing with the intention of faking or elaborating experience' (Laski 1961:15). By means of this methodology, she distinguishes four main varieties of mystical state within the category of 'intensity ecstasy' — adamic, knowledge, knowledge-contact, and union ecstasy. In the light of our critique of model four, the following criticism of her approach is most apt. According to P. G. Moore (1973:151), the truth of her guiding principles

. . . does not warrant the rigid and atomistic view of the relationship between language and experience which Laski appears to hold in tending to treat the different types or features of linguistic expression as infallible criteria for isolating different types and features of mystical experience.

Our final instance of a model four approach occurs in an exposition of Walter Hilton's *The Ladder of Perfection* by H. P. Owen, in a context in which Owen criticizes Smart's thesis of the phenomenological unity of mysticism. Above all, Owen is concerned to criticize Smart's distinction between experience and interpretation. He argues that the close interweaving of dogma and mysticism evident in Hilton's work and in the writings of other Christian mystics counts decisively against Smart's claim that there is an experiential equality between all mystical experiences. Owen maintains that if the Christian elements are abstracted from Hilton's book nothing remains since 'the whole life of contemplation that he describes is indissolubly linked to belief in Christian doctrines, in the authority of the Church, in the objective efficacy of the sacraments, and in the necessity of acquiring the Christian virtues' (1971:36–37; there is an intimation in this passage of model five, which remains undeveloped). He continues, 'Throughout the whole of Hilton's book there is not the slightest hint of any gap between experience and interpretation, contemplation and dogma, the individual mystic and the mass of non-mystical Christians, (ibid., p. 37).

Yet, in spite of the above, Owen nevertheless admits that some parts of *The Ladder of Perfection* when considered in isolation are applicable to Advaitin mysticism. Thus, while on the one hand, one can appreciate Owen's assertion of the inseparability of experience and interpretation and thereby the implication that the interpretation does reflect the actual experience, yet, on the other hand, that there are not only passages with such a low degree of theistic ramification that they are compatible with Advaitin mysticism, but also passages with a markedly high degree of Christian ramification, would appear to be an argument for Smart's thesis as much as it is an argument against it.

The difficulties involved in trying to resolve the conflict between proponents of a model four and a model two (i.e. Smartian) approach may be exemplified by considering a passage from *The Ladder of Perfection* (quoted in Owen 1971:31–32):

The third degree of contemplation, which is the highest attainable in this life, consists of both knowledge and love; that is, in knowing God and loving him perfectly. This is achieved when the soul is restored to the likeness of Jesus and filled with all virtues. It is then endowed with grace, detached from all earthly and carnal affections, and from all unprofitable thoughts and considerations of created things, and is caught up out of its bodily senses. The grace of God then illumines the mind to see all truth — that is, God — and spiritual things in him with a soft, sweet, burning love. So perfectly is this effected that for a while the soul becomes united to God in an ecstasy of love, and is conformed to the likeness of the Trinity. . . . whenever a soul is united to God in this ecstasy of love, then God and the soul are no longer two, but one: not indeed in nature, but in spirit. In this union a true marriage is made between God and the soul which shall never be broken.

Certainly it can be argued that the close interpenetration of experience and dogma in this passage is quite apparent. Thus, the soul is restored to the likeness of Jesus, endowed with grace, and conformed to the likeness of the Trinity in an ecstasy of love, etc. By contrast, the statements that the soul is 'detached from all earthly and carnal affections', 'caught up out of its bodily senses', and 'united to God' so that 'God and the soul are no longer two, but one' are applicable to many forms of mysticism. Now Owen argues that, 'the context shows that both the conceptual meaning and the experiential reference of these expressions are exclusively theistic and Christo-centric' (ibid., p. 37). But, this is not sufficient for it is merely to beg the question as to the grounds of the context, that is, that it *is* experience-based and not due to extra-experiential and post-experiential ramification. Let us consider the penultimate sentence of the above-quoted passage and ask why a distinction is made between God and the soul in *nature* while their identity in spirit is allowed. It is plausible to suggest, as Smart might, that the mystic is striving to assert the undifferentiated nature of the mystical experience and thereby wishes to evince the experiential identity of God and the soul, and yet is constrained by a doctrinal tradition which demands their ontological separateness. From this perspective, the expression 'not indeed in nature, but in spirit' is the compromise necessitated by the demands of the mystical experience and doctrinal orthodoxy. In short, therefore, there is a plausibility about both Owen's and Smart's positions. Criteria for determining which position is the more plausible are not however so easily discovered. Exegesis of mystical texts cannot help us here, for such exegesis is itself dependent upon presuppositions as to the relationship of mystical experience and its interpretation.

Discussion of a possible Smartian interpretation of the above passage leads us to a discussion of model two of which two representative proponents are Smart and Radhakrishnan. We have seen earlier in this study that Radhakrishnan's utilization of this model suffers from being committed to a normative stance, specifically, to the absolutism of the neo-Vedāntin school. Smart certainly adopts a neutral stance with respect to the relationship of mystical experience to religious doctrines in the sense that while certain forms of religious doctrine (for example, those of Theravāda Buddhism or Sānkhya) have a greater claim to congruence with mystical experience than other forms (for example, orthodox Judaism or Islam), such other forms may have a greater claim to congruence with theistic experience. Still, while Smart's proposal is a plausible alternative to models three and four, there is nothing inexorably persuasive about it unless one deifies the Ockhamistic principle of parsimony.

Nonetheless, model two is suggested in a large number of studies of mysticism. It is interesting, for example, to compare the position of several important accounts of Islamic mysticism with our earlier examination of the accounts of Fakhry and Schimmel. In the Introduction to his *Sufism* (1950:11), A. J. Arberry gives a somewhat theistic version of model two. 'It has become a platitude', he writes, 'to observe that mysticism is essentially one and the same whatever may be the religion professed by the individual mystic'. And, he continues, 'while mysticism is undoubtedly a universal constant, its variations can be observed to be very clearly and characteristically shaped by the several religious systems upon which they were based' (ibid., p. 12). It is accepted also as an unquestioned presupposition by R. A. Nicholson in his account of Islamic mysticism (1963:2):

It may be said, truly enough, that all mystical experiences meet in a single point; but that point assumes widely different aspects according to the mystic's religion, race, and temperament, while the converging lines of approach admit of almost infinite variety.

We can find it entailed too by Margaret Smith's several accounts (1976, 1977) of Christian, Islamic, and Eastern mysticism. Mysticism, according to her, is that universal tendency which transcends the very concrete traditions in which it is manifested. And the eirenic D. T. Suzuki affirms model two quite explicitly in reference to Christian and Buddhist mysticism in his comparative analysis of Eckhart and Zen Buddhism, not as the conclusion of his study but more as a presupposition of it. After considering a number of texts from the writings of Eckhart, he observes (1957:8; see also, Johnston 1978:61),

It is when I encounter such statements as these that I grow firmly convinced that the Christian experiences are not after all different from those of the Buddhist. Terminology is all that divides us and stirs us up to a wasteful dissipation of energy.

Finally, another theistic variation upon model two, and an interesting contrast to H. P. Owen's analysis, is that of Evelyn Underhill. We have already referred to her claim that there is a subtle interplay between experience and interpretation. Further to this, she maintains that mystics have recourse to two main forms of symbolic expression — the transcendent-metaphysical and the intimate-personal:

The metaphysical mystic, for whom the Absolute is impersonal and transcendent, describes his final attainment of the Absolute as *deification*, or the utter transmutation of the self in God. . . . The mystic for whom intimate and personal communion has been the mode under which he best apprehended Reality, speaks of the consummation of this communion, its perfect and permanent form, as the *Spiritual Marriage* of his soul with God. Obviously, both these terms are but the self's guesses concerning the intrinsic character of a state which it has felt in its wholeness rather than analysed. (Underhill 1930:415)

It appears from this passage that Underhill accepts that there is one form of mystical experience and two different ways of describing that experience (see also, ibid., pp. 78–79, 96, 128–129). Furthermore, she maintains that both descriptions are valid ones. Of the metaphysical mode of expression, she writes (ibid., p. 419),

Whilst the more clear-sighted are careful to qualify it in a sense which excludes pantheistic interpretations, and rebut the accusation that extreme mystics preach the annihilation of the self and regard themselves as co-equal with the Deity, they leave us in no doubt that it answers to a definite and normal experience of many souls who attain high levels of spiritual vitality. Its terms are chiefly used by those mystics by whom Reality is apprehended as a state or place rather than a Person.

However, Underhill leaves us in no doubt that she believes that the intimate-personal description is fuller and more complete as a description of mystical experience. Thus, she claims that (ibid., p. 425)

... even the most 'transcendental' mystic is constantly compelled to fall back on the language of love in the endeavour to express the content of his metaphysical raptures: and forced in the end to acknowledge that the perfect union of Lover and Beloved cannot be suggested in the precise and arid terms of religious philosophy.

Ninian Smart (1958:143) wishes to argue that Underhill has failed to give any reasons why one mystic will use a 'metaphysical' description and another will use a 'personal' description. In fact, Underhill does give a reason why metaphysical mystics revert to personal terms, a reason which supports one of Smart's central theses and delineates her position quite clearly from that of Owen:

In the last resort, the doctrine of the Incarnation is the only safeguard of the mystics against the pantheism to which they always tend. The Unconditioned Absolute, so soon as it alone becomes the object of their contemplation, is apt to be merely conceived as Divine Essence; the idea of Personality evaporates. The union of the soul with God is then thought of in terms of absorption. The distinction between Creator and creature is obliterated and loving communion is at an end. This is probably the reason why many of the greatest contemplatives ... have found that deliberate meditation upon the humanity of Christ ... was a necessity if they were to retain a healthy and well-balanced inner life. (Underhill 1930: 120–121)[7]

Underhill, therefore, in agreement with Smart and in contradistinction to Owen, maintains that personalist descriptions of mystical experience are dependent upon extra-experiential factors, that is, in Smartian terms, the necessity for Christian mystics to keep the theistic strand predominant over the mystical strand.

In the course of this chapter, we have examined four of the five models of the relationship between mystical experience and its interpretation outlined at its beginning. It has been our contention that none of these models are to be preferred. While arguments may be mounted to the effect that one has a greater degree of plausibility than another, such arguments have been found to be unpersuasive. Thus, models three and four appear to give a better account of the variety of mystical utterance as against models one or two. On the other hand, model two in its Smartian form and in conjunction with its emphasis on the theistic strand is able to both recognize the complexity of religious expressions and combine these with a parsimonious account of religious experience. Nevertheless, all these models finally fail to persuade that they have bridged the 'ineffability gap' between experience and interpretation. Crucial to this whole study therefore is the delineation of a means whereby this gap might be, if not bridged, then at least narrowed. And this shall be our concern in the next chapter when we examine model five.

8

The Varieties of Mystical Experience:
A Philosophical Prolegomenon

During the course of this study, one particular question has periodically arisen and just as periodically been postponed for later discussion. This has been the question of firstly, the possibility of, and therefore secondly, the question of the occurrence of mystical experience of a theistic kind. The necessity of such a postponement has perhaps been demonstrated by our discussion in the last chapter. In short, rejection of the possibility of and therefore the occurrence of such experience cannot be said to have been persuasively demonstrated by Radhakrishnan, Smart, or Stace. On the other hand, Zaehner and a number of proponents of model four have attempted to demonstrate that such theistic mystical experiences do occur. Nevertheless, because it has been argued that the extrapolation from a particular form of mystical utterance to its being the reflection of a particular form of mystical experience is fraught with a number of problems, it has not been demonstrated that such experiences occur although it must be conceded that such analyses reinforce the possibility of their occurrence.

In this chapter, we shall be particularly concerned with this question. Firstly, we shall be concerned with the possibility of its occurrence, and then, by an analysis of model five, as adumbrated in the first section of the last chapter, with its actual occurrence. By means of a number of criticisms of model five, we shall also hope to demonstrate the possibility of discriminating between different states or levels of mystical experience. We shall begin our discussion by considering a critique of Smart's thesis of the phenomenological identity of mystical experience offered by Nelson Pike.

In an important reply to Ninian Smart's 'Interpretation and Mystical Experience' (1965a) Nelson Pike (1965) sets out to argue that it is possible to delineate experiences which are phenomenologically theistic mystical, experiences which may minimally be said to be 'self in contact with another' and maximally 'the union of the soul with God'. In support of his thesis, Pike examines two passages purportedly reporting such mystical experiences, the first from James's *Varieties of Religious Experience*, the second from Jan van Ruysbroeck's *The Adornment of the Spiritual Marriage*.

The first of these passages reads as follows (James 1961:64, quoted in Pike 1965:146):

There was not a mere consciousness of something there, but fused in the central happiness of it, a startling awareness of some ineffable good. Not vague either, not like the emotional effect of some poem, or scene or blossom, of music, but the sure knowledge of the close presence of a sort of mighty person, and after it went, the memory persisted as the one perception of reality. Everything else might be a dream, but not that.

Pike argues that in this passage, the reporter seems to be clearly saying that the experience was (phenomenologically) one in which he was aware of another. Hence, he maintains, '. . . the description of the experience as "self in contact with God" mentions nothing other than the explicit content of the experience' (ibid., p. 146).

The crucial problem with utilizing the above account as indicative of mystical experience is the fact that the experience of which it is expressive cannot be said to be clearly mystical at all. It may appear from this comment that I have some secret knowledge, hitherto undisclosed, of the necessary features of mystical experience. In order to allay this appearance, a number of points may be apposite. Firstly, therefore, while James remarks that it would not be unnatural to deem it as a *theistic* experience, it is not delineated by James (1961:64) as a *mystical* one, nor does the recipient deem it as such. Secondly, the recipient himself does not even interpret the experience theistically. Thus phenomenologically, it ought not to be viewed as 'the union of the soul with God'. Thirdly, it is even phenomenologically a slim candidate for 'self in contact with another'. There is certainly a sense of the self aware of the presence of another but there is no implication of contact with another in the Plotinian sense of 'contact with the One'.[1] This point is further reinforced by the fact that James reports (1961:63–64) that the same person has been subject to other experiences of the awareness of another in which the latter assumes an evil, if not demonic form. Fourthly, if we do consider the experience as a theistic experience of some sort or another, then it bears closer analogies to those experiences which we have delineated earlier in this study as *theistic* experiences than to those passages putatively expressive of *theistic mystical* experience. In his reply to Pike, Smart remarks (1965b:156),

I would not deny that, in the William James case cited by Mr. Pike, the sense of 'another' is part of the phenomenology. Indeed it is characteristic of prophetism, *bhakti*, and their analogues to involve a 'numinous' type of experience in which a gap, so to say, exists between the Other and the worshipper.

While therefore the case is dubious with respect to Pike's first example, the passage from *The Adornment of The Spiritual Marriage* is much more clearly a mystical utterance. Pike quotes van Ruysbroeck to this effect (1965:148):

And the bare, uplifted memory feels itself enwrapped and established in an abysmal Absence of Image. And thereby the created image is united above reason in a threefold way with its Eternal Image, which is the origin of its being and its life; and this origin is preserved and possessed, essentially and eternally, through a simple seeing in an imageless void; and so a man is lifted up above reason in a threefold manner into the Unity, and in a onefold manner into the Trinity. Yet the creature does not become God, for the union takes place in God through grace and our homeward-turning love: and therefore the creature in its inward contemplation feels a distinction and an otherness between itself and God. . . . There [in the mystic state] all is full and overflowing, for the spirit feels itself to be one truth and one richness and one unit with God. Yet even here there is an essential tending toward, and therein is an essential distinction between the being of the soul and the Being of God; and this is the highest and finest distinction which we are able to feel.

I have quoted this passage *in extenso* because I believe it to be a particularly clear example of a first-order mystical text outlining the nature of a mystical experience. Moreover, there is an overt claim that, at the height of mystical union with God, there is nonetheless a recognition of the ultimate separateness of God and the soul. The assertion that, even in oneness, there is 'tending toward' separateness does appear to be a claim reflecting the experience itself and not necessitated by an extra-experiential doctrine. Indeed, it is clearly stated that the creature *feels* a distinction between itself and God. A difference between the self and God is actually experienced; no subsequent reflection here!

Let us, however, turn to Smart's remarks upon this passage. He argues firstly, that the passage 'for the Spirit feels itself to be one truth and one richness and one unit with God' is evidence that Ruysbroeck's experience is one of undifferentiated unity; and secondly, that those passages which speak of the difference of the soul and God do not relate to the pinnacle of mystical experience but are expressive of an immediate awareness of the past, before union eventuated, and an immediate anticipation of the cessation of union. Thus, of the section dealing with the 'tending toward', he writes (1965b:157),

Now it is characteristic of contemplative experience that the 'subject-object' distinction does not apply — it is not like being here and seeing a flower over there, etc. On the other hand, in so far as there is an awareness on the part of the contemplative of where he has come from in arriving at the mystical experience, there is a sense of 'tending toward'. . . The point can be paralleled very clearly in the Buddhist *jhānas* or stages of contemplation, where the sense of achievement in arriving at the higher contemplative state has to be set aside; i.e., one has to go on until there is no awareness of 'tending toward', as there is no awareness of the environment, etc.

Now I would not wish to deny that in Buddhism at the attainment of the highest mystical state, there is no sense of 'tending toward'. Nor would I deny that the same is applicable in some Christian mystics, for example, St. John of the Cross (see Gibbs 1976:537). However, to argue, as Smart appears to do, that because there is no sense of 'tending toward' in Buddhism, there is no sense of 'tending toward' in the experience of van Ruysbroeck is merely to beg the question as to the nature of the experiences; it is to assume that they are to be treated as phenomenologically identical. Indeed, unless one were to come to the passage from van Ruysbroeck with a predilection in favour of Smart's thesis, the far more probable exegesis of the passage would be to see it as reflective, not of an experience of undifferentiated unity, but rather of the unity of the soul and God (phenomenologically speaking).

To be sure, the conflict between Smart and Pike is very much an exegetical one, and although the passage from van Ruysbroeck is a better contender as a reflection of theistic mystical experience than the passage from Walter Hilton utilized by Owen, it would be premature to assert that our exegesis of this text is obviously preferable to Smart's. Nevertheless, Pike does make several methodological points which may lead us towards a clarification, if not a resolution of such conflicts.

' The first of these is somewhat negative. It is to the effect that the recognition that an experience is phenomenologically one of the soul in union with God does not entail a commitment to a claim about the existence of God. Although, in general, such existence claims may be generated by or reinforced by such experiences, there is nothing contradictory about affirming the experience as one in which the recipient felt himself to be unified with God and then denying the existence of God. Pike claims, quite correctly, that this is to do no more than to acknowledge the experience as hallucinatory. He remarks, 'As long as the description is offered as a purely phenomenological account of the content of the experience, it involves no ontological commitment on the part of the one offering the description' (1965:147).

Of course, to the extent that any purely phenomenological account is ramified by extra-experiential doctrines, the truth of which are accepted by the interpreter, then to that extent also ontological commitment may be present. As we have seen clearly in an earlier chapter, Zaehner does tend to slide from phenomenological analysis to ontological commitment. Nevertheless, Pike's point that the recognition that there can be phenomenologically theistic mystical experiences does not necessitate ontological commitment remains an important one. The recognition of such experiences does not thereby invalidate the neutrality of our account.

Pike's second point is of great significance and I shall therefore quote it in full. Of the reporter of the experience detailed by James, he writes (1965:146-147),

Let us suppose that he was a committed Christian prior to his experience. One might hold that the fact that he experienced himself in contact with a good and mighty person was in some way determined by his prior theological beliefs. Had he not believed in the existence of God, he would not have experienced himself in contact with such a person. Let us grant this. The description of the experience as 'Self in contact with God' would still be a purely phenomenological description. Prior to his dream, my son believed that Paul Bunyan's ox was blue. As a consequence, he dreamed of himself riding on a *blue* ox. But that the dream-ox was experienced as *blue* is part of the phenomenological description of that dream. It is not an item my son incorporated into the description of the dream after waking, as a consequence of his belief that the ox was blue.

There are a number of issues implicit within this passage which merit further development. Firstly, there is the question of the possible points at which interpretation may occur. There are three possibilities: After the experience (through reflection upon it); during the experience; and prior to the experience (by shaping the nature of the experience). These may be called 'retrospective', 'reflexive', and 'incorporated' interpretation respectively. (I owe the terminology to Moore 1973:147-148.) With reference therefore to the dream of the young Pike, his prior belief that the ox was blue is incorporated into the dream (incorporated interpretation) such that he sees the ox as a blue ox during the dream (reflexive interpretation) and upon waking describes his dream as that of riding on a blue ox (retrospective interpretation). A theistic mystical experience on this frame of reference is one in which a prior belief in God is incorporated into the mystical experience such that during it the self is aware of contact with another and subsequently describes that experience as one of union with God. We shall return to this anon. For the present, however, and arising from this, we may note the existence of an implicit model of the relationship between mystical experience and its interpretation, namely model five, the view that there are as many varieties of mystical experience as there are *incorporated interpretations* of it.

In our earlier analysis of model four, we saw that the central problem was one of circularity. That is to say, the view that there are as many varieties of mystical experience as there are paradigmatic expressions of it *assumed* that the paradigmatic expressions 'pictured' the nature of the experience. Model five avoids this problem since what we may now call 'paradigmatic symbols' enter into the structure and content of the experience itself. And I use the word 'symbols' to indicate that not only beliefs and doctrines, but also the symbolism of art and architecture, social customs and structures too, may be incorporated. Thus, the 'ineffability gap', the barrier between interpretation and experience is, to that extent, narrowed.

The earliest occurrence of an implicit commitment to model five of which I am aware is in Rufus Jones's *Studies in Mystical Religion* in 1909. The basic thrust of the assumption upon which he operates is best expressed in the following passage (p. xxxiv):

There are no 'pure experiences', i.e. no experiences which come wholly from *beyond* the person who has them. ... The most refined mysticism, the most exalted spiritual experience is *partly* a product of the social and intellectual environment in which the personal life of the mystic has formed and matured. There are no experiences of any sort which are independent of preformed expectations or unaffected by the prevailing beliefs of the time. ... Mystical experiences will be, perforce, saturated with the dominant ideas of the group to which the mystic belongs, and they will reflect the expectations of that group and that period.

A more explicit defence of model five is offered by Bruce Garside in an article entitled 'Language and the Interpretation of Mystical Experience' (1972). According to Garside, experience in general is a product of the interaction between the organism and its environment. He contends that the more we move away from perceptions of physical bodies to perceptions related to other people, to moral and aesthetic judgements, to perceptions of 'inner' states, the more determinative are the peculiarities of especial cultural and conceptual frameworks. Accordingly, mystical experience, being about as far as possible removed from the perception of physical objects, is most likely a highly socialized experience. For Garside then, the phenomenology of the mystical experience is almost totally dependent upon the incorporated interpretation. Indeed, from the perspective of his position the distinction between experience and interpretation is virtually a nugatory one:

If experience is the product of stimuli and conceptual framework as suggested above, then people of different cultures and different religious traditions would necessarily have different religious experiences. It makes no sense to look for an 'authentic' description of a mystical experience 'undistorted' by any interpretive framework. (Garside 1972:99)

Garside's suggestion, that the relationship between mystical experience and its interpretation bears some analogies to the relationship between experience in general and the interpretation of it, is developed much more fully by Steven Katz. His investigation of mystical experience is based upon the single epistemological assumption that there are no pure (i.e. unmediated) experiences. Thus, he writes, 'This "mediated" aspect of all our experience seems an inescapable feature of any epistemological inquiry, including the inquiry into mysticism, which has to be properly acknowledged if our investigation of experience, including mystical experience, is to get very far' (1978:26).

Katz, in fact, stands quite firmly as the leading proponent of model five. Thus, he contends that in order to understand mysticism we must not merely examine retrospective interpretations but also acknowledge that both the experience and the form in which it is reported are shaped by concepts which the mystic brings to his experience:

... the forms of consciousness which the mystic brings to experience set structured and limiting parameters on what the experience will be, i.e. on what will be experienced, and rule out in advance what is 'inexperienceable' in the particular given, concrete, context. Thus, for example, the nature of the Christian mystic's pre-mystical consciousness informs the mystical consciousness such that he experiences the mystic reality in terms of Jesus, the Trinity, or a personal God, etc., rather than in terms of the non-personal, non-everything, to be precise, Buddhist doctrine of nirvāṇa. (Katz 1978:26–27; see also, Eliade 1965:77)

Quite clearly, the discussion of model five, in these terms, places a quite fresh perspective on our whole discussion of theistic mystical experience. Indeed, not only is the possibility of such experiences delineated, but their actual occurrence appears certain. Thus, with respect to Jewish mystical experience, Katz contends that the entire life of the Jewish mystic is saturated from childhood onwards by images, concepts, symbols, and rituals which define in advance the experience he wishes to have and thereby determine what the experience will be like. Thus, he writes (1978:34),

. . . the Jewish conditioning pattern so strongly impresses that tradition's mystics (as all Jews) with the fact that one does *not* have mystical experiences of God in which one loses one's identity in ecstatic moments of unity, that the Jewish mystic rarely, if ever, has such experiences. What the Jewish mystic experiences is, perhaps, the Divine Throne, or the angel Metatron, or aspects of the *Sefiroth*, or the heavenly court and palaces, or the Hidden Torah, or God's secret Names, but not loss of self in unity with God.

Clearly, this model of the relationship between mystical experience and its interpretation is epistemologically a far more subtle one than any we have examined heretofore. And, if we adopt it, a number of advantages accrue. Firstly, we are able to take into account the plurality of mystical utterances. Model five entails, in effect, that there are a wide variety of phenomenologically disparate mystical experiences due, in the main, to the conceptual and cultural settings in which they have their origin. And therefore, with reference to the exegesis of retrospective interpretations, we avoid the problem of having to accommodate such interpretations to the demands of an *a priori* theory of the nature of mystical experience. Rather, this model suggests that there will be a correspondence between a mystical experience which incorporates a particular conceptual and cultural set and a retrospective interpretation which reflects that same set. That is to say, there will be a correlation between the incorporated interpretation, the mystical experience, and the retrospective interpretation.

The adoption of model five implies consequently a thorough-going contextualist approach to the study of mysticism. Negatively, this means that those studies of mysticism which extrapolate from the content of mystical utterances to the nature of the experiences which they reflect without taking into account the possible ways in which the experience itself is informed by the mystics' cultural sets are methodologically unsound. Positively, it means that attention needs to be focused on the total cultural milieu in which the experience occurs. The catch-cry of model five is, so to say, 'Away from the universal, and towards the particular!'

It would though be premature to extrapolate from the details of the earlier quoted passage from van Ruysbroeck to an assertion of the actual nature of the experience upon which it is based. To be sure, in the light of the fact that it is a first-order mystical utterance, and as a result of model five, it would not be inappropriate to conclude that the experience to which it refers is a theistic mystical one. But before that could be guaranteed, a number of tasks would need to be performed. On the one hand, careful study of the paradigmatic concepts and symbols of van Ruysbroeck's tradition would be essential to understanding the content of the experience. And, on the other hand, attention would still need to be paid to the possibility of the ramification of the retrospective interpretation by factors not incorporated into the experience, for these may still play a role in such interpretations. Our earlier exegesis of Walter Hilton's 'not indeed in nature, but in spirit' could be viewed as an example of such a process.

A further factor is perhaps of even more importance. We have seen that model five implies that the mystical experience will *necessarily* reflect the interpretation incorporated into it. We must, however, be wary of too strict an interpretation of the dependence of mystical experiences on the context out of which they arise. For if we maintain that there is a connection between the nature of the experience and the context that informs it such that the former is *necessarily* determined by the latter, then it is impossible to account for those experiences which go beyond or are at odds with the received context. To be sure, mysticism may have, and often does have, a conservative ambience. The mystic may experientially reaffirm, or even 'verify', the tradition in which he operates. And the epistemological grounds for the conservative character of the mystical experience are given by model five. The mystic's experience reaffirms the tradition because the paradigmatic symbols of it are incorporated into the experience.

The determinative effect of the pre-experiential content is also reinforced by considering the role, on the mystic way, of the teacher or spiritual guide of a specific path and a specific goal. Thus, in Kabbalism, in Sūfism, in Buddhism, in Hinduism, and in Christianity, the role of the teacher is crucial, both as the guide to the path and the judge of the student's progress along it. The function of the teacher is, in part, psychological. For he prevents the student from straying into dangerous psychological states. But more significant is his sociological function. The teacher guides the student into experiences that reinforce the tradition, for he represents (in some cases, is) the religious authority.

But all this does not entail that the mystic cannot experientially go beyond the received tradition. Within the Christian tradition, for example, it was variance with the received tradition which necessitated the delineation of criteria for discriminating between divine and satanic experiences. St. Teresa of Avila, for example, offers two such criteria. The first is that the experience must be generative of religious values — humility, love, trust, etc. (Peers 1960:237). The second is that the experience must be compatible with the content of Scripture. Thus, she writes (ibid., p. 239),

As far as I can see and learn by experience, the soul must be convinced that a thing comes from God only if it is in conformity with Holy Scripture; if it were to diverge from that in the very least, I think I should be incomparably more firmly convinced that it came from the devil than I previously was that it came from God, however sure I might have felt of this.

A mystical experience may lead too to the creative transformation of a religious tradition. Mystical experience is capable of generating new interpretations of the tradition while yet remaining faithful to it. Thus for example, as Gershom Scholem points out, the Kabbalist Isaac Luria 'fully accepted the established religious authority, which indeed he undertook to reinforce by enhancing its stature and giving it deeper meaning' (Scholem 1965:21). He continues, 'the ideas he employed in this seemingly conservative task were utterly new and seem doubly daring in their conservative context' (ibid.).

The teachings of Meister Eckhart in the Christian tradition and al Hallāj in the Islamic tradition also appear to reflect experiences, the interpretations of which signal a move beyond the limits of what was acceptable to their respective traditions. And the accounts of the Buddha's quest for enlightenment and his enlightenment experience may also reflect the incompatibility between his experience and the received tradition of Hinduism.

In sum then, even if we grant the cogency of model five, we must be wary of too crude an application of it. The nature of the experience cannot be read solely from the supposed incorporated content. Again, only contextual analysis in particular cases will determine the interplay between experience, incorporated, and retrospective interpretation.

But it can of course be argued that what appear to be exceptions to model five are not really exceptions at all because *all* mystical experiences *necessarily*, by definition, reflect some form of incorporated interpretation. Thus there is no conflict between the nature of the experience and the received tradition, so such an argument would go, but rather between the received tradition and another tradition incorporated into the experience at odds with the received tradition. Thus, Katz for example, appears to maintain that model five is true *a priori*, and that therefore there cannot *logically* be any contrary cases.

The empirical quest for contrary cases is of no avail in this case. That is to say, the search for mystical experiences the retrospective interpretations of which appear to conflict with the context out of which they arose is a logically improper one. The advocate of the necessary truth of model five will argue that the contents of the experience *must* reflect some incorporated interpretation even if no evidence of such an interpretation can be found, even if the contents of the experience conflict with the received tradition, and so on. In short, necessary truths are not amenable to empirical falsification.

But such an *a priori* position is *logically* assailable if it can be shown that it is logically possible that there are experiences in which there is no incorporated interpretation *at all*; and to this question we may now turn.

Model five, as outlined above, is in direct conflict with the Smartian thesis that there is a phenomenological unity in mystical experience. That is to say, if incorporated interpretation does occur, then Smart's thesis is false, and vice versa. And yet, surprisingly enough, Smart himself apparently sees no conflict between this notion of incorporated interpretation and his own notion of the unity of mystical experience. Let us recall a passage from Smart which I quoted earlier (1965a:79, my italics):

It is to be noted [he writes] that ramifications may enter into the descriptions either because of the intentional nature of the experience or through reflection upon it. Thus a person brought up in a Christian environment and strenuously practising the Christian life may have a contemplative experience which he sees *as* a union with God. *The whole spirit of his quest will affect the way he sees his experience; or, to put it another way, the whole spirit of his quest will enter into the experience.* On the other hand, a person might only come to see the experience in this way after the event, as it were: upon reflection he interprets his experience in theological categories.

Certainly, in this passage, Smart recognizes the possibility of both incorporated and retrospective interpretation, and, more significantly, the possibility of *theistic* incorporated interpretation. Similarly, in his rejoinder to Pike, he writes (1965b:157), 'I do not deny that theological notions may enter into the phenomenology of an experience. Theological notions in this way need not be extra-experiential'.

Again, surprisingly, he continues (ibid.), 'But this does not affect my central thesis [*viz.* of the phenomenological unity of mystical experience]. Consider feelings in the chest: they can be felt as pangs of indigestion. But a doctor could say: "These feelings arise from fluid in the lungs".'

His rejoinder to Pike reiterates the fact that Smart perceives no conflict between models two and five. But the medical analogy gives a hint as to the reason for this. It is unfortunate that the analogy is not as clear as it might be, and moreover, is not elaborated further in the text of his rejoinder, nor is it or a similar analogy to be found in any of Smart's other published writings. Nevertheless, there is the suggestion in this analogy that, just as the individual who feels pains in his chest incorrectly diagnoses them as pangs of indigestion, so also the theistic mystic who sees his experience as a union with God has made a similar mistake. Only on this interpretation of the medical analogy can we make sense of Smart's claim that the recognition of incorporated interpretation does not affect his central thesis. And yet, quite clearly, if there is incorporated interpretation such that the mystic sees the experience as one of union with God, and reports it as such, then he does not appear to have made a mistake comparable with the mistaken medical analysis. Having registered the fact that the analogy, at least when viewed in this way, does not seem to support Smart's thesis against the recognized possibility of incorporated interpretation, the question remains as to why Smart believes that it *does* so support it. One feels inclined to say that our disposal of the medical analogy was just a little too simple, and therefore, one ought to look for a deeper level to Smart's apparent non-perceiving of the conflict between models two and five. I shall now attempt to suggest that there are reasons why Smart does not perceive the conflict. And further, I shall argue that these reasons do not support either models two or five. Indeed, from our discussion, we shall hope to generate the outlines of a further model of the relationship between mystical experience and its interpretation.

It is important to recognize that in those passages in which the notion of incorporated interpretation is adverted to by Smart, and in the medical analogy, there is reference to the concept of 'experiencing-as' — specifically, 'seeing-as' and 'feeling-as'. There is no explanation of Smart's intention in using these phrases in his writings. Nevertheless, we shall take these phrases as clues towards the discernment of such an intention.

The notion with which we are about to deal is by now, at least in other contexts, a familiar one, having been brought to not some little clarity by Wittgenstein in his *Philosophical Investigations* (1972:193). Suffice it to say therefore, that in his discussion of 'seeing-as', Wittgenstein pointed to ambiguous diagrams such as the Necker cube, Jastrow's duck-rabbit, and Köhler's goblet-faces. Thus, for example, Köhler's diagram can be seen as the outline of a goblet, or as two faces looking at each other. The duck-rabbit can be seen as a duck's head facing to the right or as a rabbit's head facing to the left, etc. In other words, we may speak of a perception as 'seeing-as' when what is received by the senses can be consciously perceived in different ways, as having a different character, nature, significance, etc. In short, the received sensations are identical, the apparent perceptions are varied.

Let us assume that Smart is using this notion in an analogous sense to that outlined above. In this case then, it could be postulated that, on the one hand, all mystical 'sensations' are the same in all cases (model two), while, on the other hand, mystical 'perceptions' are varied as a result of the incorporated interpretations. In other words, we might be able to suggest that there are varied contents in mystical experiences, not because there are varied 'perceptions' of different mystical objects, but because the *apparent* 'perceptions' are varied as a consequence of the various incorporated interpretations. The same mystical 'sensations' lie behind the conflicting apparent 'perceptions'.

In order to explore this suggestion more closely, we may invoke the previously outlined notion of 'reflexive interpretation'. According to that, interpretation may take place during the experience itself. Thus, with reference to experience in general, seeing a configuration of lines as, on the one hand, a goblet or, on the other, as a pair of faces looking at each other is a case of reflexive interpretation. So also, 'seeing' a mystical experience *as* a union with God is also a case of reflexive interpretation, the nature of the reflexivity being determined by the incorporated belief. And here we may discern a clue as to when it is necessary to distinguish between reflexive interpretation and the possible object of it. That is, where the reflexive interpreting is in part (at least) dependent upon incorporated interpretation, we can distinguish in principle between the interpreting of the experience and the possible object of the thus-interpreted experience. This should not be taken as an argument against the possible existence of any object thus experienced. Rather, it is merely to maintain that the 'perceptual load' which any such apparently perceived object carries is determined not by the object itself, but by what the mystic brings to the experience through incorporated interpretation.

In the light of the above suggestion, it may now be clear why Smart does not perhaps view his thesis of the unity of mystical experience as incompatible with model five. For, granted that there is incorporated interpretation such that there may be phenomenologically theistic mystical experiences, the notion of reflexive interpretation indicates that during mystical experience, or at least during those mystical experiences in which there is some phenomenological content, there may be interpretation of a yet more basic datum of experience, just as, in the cases of the diagrams mentioned above, there is reflexive interpretation of the basic data of certain configurations of lines.

I think that if we understand Smart in this way, then we have done greater justice to his writings than would have been the case had we merely registered the apparent conflict in his writings between models two and five and not proceeded further. Nevertheless, there is implicit within our above discussion another model of the relationship between mystical experience and its interpretation, a model which hopefully takes the insights of both models two and five, and points towards a fresh synthesis.

From our analysis of model five, we have seen that it is not only possible but is indeed most likely that theistic mystical experiences occur. If a theistic conceptual and symbolic framework is incorporated into the mystical experience then, in spite of the presence of reflexive interpretation, the mystical experience may be said to be *phenomenologically* one of the union of the soul and God. Nevertheless, this does not necessitate the adoption of model five, for the possibility of reflexive interpretation leads to the notion of extrapolating a core mystical datum from the experience, a datum which may well be experientially realized in some mystical experiences.

Let us now turn to this notion of the core-datum of mystical experience and attempt to outline what such a core-datum might be like and how we might set about identifying it. If we turn firstly to the cases of the duck-rabbit, etc., the core-datum is easily identifiable. In short, the core-datum is the configuration of lines in each case. Indeed, in these cases, there is *seeing-as* only because it is quite apparent that the seeing of the diagrams as configurations of lines is quite separate from seeing them *as* a duck or rabbit, a goblet or faces, etc. In other words, there is neither a conceptual nor an actual difficulty in seeing the configuration of lines, *qua seeing*, as a configuration of lines, and seeing the configuration of lines, *qua seeing-as*, as duck or rabbit, goblet or faces, etc. The case of dreams is somewhat more murky. To revert to the dream of the blue ox, can it be said that reflexive interpretation is taking place? If the answer is yes, then what remains as the basic datum of dream experience if the contents of the dream are 'bracketed out' as due to incorporated interpretation? The apparent datum would appear to be a dream-state without content.

To be sure, the abstraction of the content of dreams from the dream-state renders the word 'dream' meaningless in these circumstances for 'a dream without content' appears to have no application. Nevertheless, this does not negate the fact that there is a state equivalent to a contentless dream-state, namely, the state of dreamless sleep, and, at least in some sense of the word 'experience', an experience of dreamless sleep (for one is aware afterwards that one has had it). Now in the mystical case, and taking a theistic mystical experience as our example, what remains as the basic datum of the mystical experience if the content of the experience, the experience of the self in union with God, is abstracted? The residue is a contentless experience, one in which there is neither awareness of the self (of normal consciousness) nor of 'anything' standing over against the self — a state in which, unlike the waking and the dream-state, there is no subject-object polarity. It is, furthermore, a state in which there is neither incorporated paradigmatic beliefs or symbols, nor, *ergo*, reflexive interpretation, for there are no beliefs, thoughts, symbols, dual awareness therein. In other words, it is a state in which the distinctions between the knower, the act of knowing, and what is known are obliterated.

There is nothing logically incoherent about the notion of a contentless experience. And it is therefore logically possible that there are experiences in which there is no incorporated interpretation. If this is so, then the view that all mystical experiences reflect some form of incorporated interpretation cannot be held to be true *a priori*. For it may be the case that some mystical experiences are experiences in which there is no incorporated interpretation, that is to say, are contentless experiences.

The above theoretical discussion now leads to the presentation of a number of hypotheses. These are as follows:
(i) The postulated datum of mystical experience *is* attained by mystics;
(ii) the limiting case of mystical experience is such a state;
(iii) the contemplative path, in some traditions, leads to the transcending of content-filled states and the attainment of the 'pure' state;
(iv) the 'pure' state is most often attained in the context of a set of doctrines appropriate to such attainment.

The full evaluation of the hypotheses presented above is not appropriate within the context of this study. This is for the reason that, as was outlined in our discussion of model five, each hypotheses would need to be examined in the total context of each mystical tradition and therefore, the evaluation of the theses needs to be carried out by specialists within each tradition. Nevertheless, perhaps it may not be altogether inappropriate to venture forth with a few suggestions as to the sort of evidence which might support these theses.

The first hypothesis is clearly the most crucial one. We may note that the contentless state to which this hypothesis refers is that upon which Stace, Smart, Otto, and Radhakrishnan base their accounts of the mystical experience. That is to say, it is precisely that state which Stace designates as the undifferentiated unity of pure consciousness, '. . . from which all the multiplicity of sensuous or conceptual or other empirical content has been excluded, so that there remains only a void and empty unity' (Stace 1961:110).

Similarly, it is to this state that Smart adverts when he says (1968:42),

In the contemplative state . . . discursive thought and mental images disappear. . . . If the contemplative experience is void of images, etc., it is also void of that sense of distinction between subject and object which characterizes everyday experience.

To be sure, the discernment of the attainment of this state of contentlessness through the analysis of mystical texts is fraught with the kinds of exegetical problems we have uncovered during the course of this study. Nevertheless, in the light of our earlier discussions, it does not seem implausible to suggest that this state is attained in the highest stages of the contemplative path in, for example, Theravāda Buddhism, Sānkhya-Yoga, and in Plotinus. Certainly, the retrospective interpretations of these traditions do vary. Yet, I can see no good reason for arguing, as perhaps Katz would, that the phenomenology of the mystical experience which generates or reinforces the doctrine of non-soul is different from that which generates or reinforces the notion of the individual *purusha*. Indeed, at this level, it is difficult to see what difference incorporated interpretation could possibly make. Thus, I cannot but agree with Smart that if the doctrine of non-soul is to be preferred to the doctrine of soul, then that preferment must be determined on grounds other than the mystical experience for both doctrines gain reinforcement from the contentless state of the mystical experience.

The occurrence of contentless experience provides therefore a counter-balance to the somewhat deterministic view of model five that *all* mystical experience is totally dependent on its context. It suggests rather that there are mystical experiences which, by virtue of their contentlessness, are identical irrespective of the cultural milieu in which they occur. In so far as we are speaking of contentless mystical experiences, there is a unanimity and a universality which transcends the cultural context in which they occur.

I do not wish to suggest that those stages of mystical experience prior to the attainment of the contentless state do not differ between traditions or even between mystics within the same tradition. For, in mystical states which are generated as a result of following a particular tradition of meditation and which are prior to the attainment of the contentless state, incorporated interpretation will play a crucial role. That is to say, these prior states will be content-filled states, the content being partly determined by the paradigmatic cultural and religious symbols incorporated into these states. Thus, for example, although the contentless and therefore final state in Theravāda Buddhism and in Yoga may be said to be phenomenologically identical, the stages of experience leading to the final state are quite clearly disparate (on the *jhānas* in Theravāda, see Buddhaghosa's *Visuddhimagga*, 2.10 (1971); and on the stages of *samādhi* in yoga, see Dasgupta 1973:150–158). So also in Plotinus, it is evident that the mystical stages on the return to the One are determined by the concepts of the outgoing of the One from itself in the process of cosmic emanation (see especially, Dodds 1960:1–7).

The recognition that, in an analysis of mystical experience, one needs to give due consideration to the stages of mystical experience attained as the mystic proceeds along the contemplative path is important for a number of reasons. Firstly, while it is recognized by Smart and, to a considerably lesser extent by Stace, that there are stages along the path, neither gives serious place in their respective analyses of mystical experience to the reports of phenomenologically distinct stages of mystical experience along the way to the highest state. For this reason, their delineation of the nature of mystical experience is deficient, for, and this is our second reason, not only are the earlier stages of mystical experience worthy of consideration in themselves, but also, understanding of the higher stages may be facilitated by an appreciation of the preceding stages. Thus, for example, exposition of the fourth formless *jhāna* in the Theravādin tradition, the sphere of neither perception nor non-perception, cannot but be enriched by consideration of the three preceding *jhānas*, the spheres of infinite space, infinite consciousness, and nothingness. Indeed, part of the necessary technique for the attainment of the fourth formless *jhana* is meditation upon the non-ultimacy of the sphere of nothingness (Buddhaghosa, *Visuddhimagga*, 2.10.4).

Thirdly, the recognition of the stages of mystical experience gives support to our second and third hypotheses. To advert to the Theravāda tradition again, the fourth formless *jhāna* is the limiting case of mystical experience in the sense that there is no longer the awareness that there is perception of, for example, symbolic content, nor the awareness that there is no perception. A contentless state has been attained. And moreover, this state is attained in the transcending of the final content-filled state, the sphere of nothingness, however shadowy and elusive that content may appear to be. To quote Buddhaghosa (ibid.),

Who so has reached mastery over the attainment of the sphere of nothingness in these five ways, and wishes to develop the sphere of neither perception nor non-perception, should first see the evils of the former sphere as, 'This attainment has the sphere of infinite consciousness for a near enemy. It is not calm like the sphere of neither perception nor non-perception. . . .' He should then put an end to hankering after it and, attending to the sphere of neither perception nor non-perception as calm, should repeatedly advert to that attainment of the sphere of nothingness which has proceeded with nothingness as object, should attend to it, reflect upon it, impinge upon it with application and exercise of thought, regarding it as calm! calm! As he repeatedly drives his mind on to the sign, the hindrances are discarded, mindfulness is established, the mind is concentrated through access.

To put it simply, the contemplative process in the Theravādin tradition consists in progressing through the four *jhānas* of form and the three formless *jhānas*, each of which is progressively less content-filled until the fourth formless *jhāna* of contentlessness is attained.[2]

The contemplative path, therefore, as exemplified by the Theravādin tradition appears to support the third hypothesis noted above, namely, that in some traditions the various content-filled states of mystical experience may be transcended and the 'pure' state attained. And the inner logic of the contemplative path suggests too that this latter state is a limiting one. That is to say, while it is always possible to pass beyond a content-filled state to a less content-filled state, the contentless state is, as it were, the upper limit of the meditative process. In other words, meditational techniques, of their nature, conduce towards the realization of the state of contentlessness.

I do not, however, wish to give the appearance of suggesting that the 'pure' state is attained in all mystical traditions. Indeed, if we are willing to take Steven Katz at his word, and there seems no reason why we shouldn't, such a contentless state is not common in the Jewish tradition of mysticism. Nevertheless, it would be remiss if we did not note that there is certainly one notable exception to this, namely, Martin Buber (see Buber 1961:42–44). For, at least in his earlier life, and perhaps because of his wide knowledge of the Hasidic tradition of mysticism, he certainly appears to be a recipient of contentless mystical experience, which he initially interpreted in a Vedāntin sense and subsequently reinterpreted in a Sānkhyin way. Furthermore, it cannot be denied that there is a constant tendency in Jewish mysticism to develop a pantheistic or at least a panentheistic theology, although only thoroughgoing contextual analysis could discern the experiential basis of such theology. (Such panentheism is most pronounced in the *Sefer Ha Zohar* or 'Book of Splendour', written in the late thirteenth century, probably by the Spanish kabbalist Moses de Leon; see Scholem 1961:156–243.)

With respect to at least some forms of the Christian mystical experience also, it seems fairly certain that the contentless state is not attained and that the essence of the mystical experience lies in the experienced union of the soul and God, or at least in an overwhelming experience of loving and being loved. We have noted the probability of the passage from van Ruysbroeck discussed earlier as reflecting just such an experience. However, even within the ambit of the Christian doctrinal framework, it is not impossible that the mystic may attain the contentless state. Thus, for example, in St. John of the Cross, all mystical visions and illuminations are rejected. That is to say, content-filled mystical experiences are rejected just because they are specific, clear, and distinct. To this extent, therefore, the mystic cannot come into conflict with the teachings of the Church for the aim of the mystic, according to St. John of the Cross, is not to gain knowledge of heavenly things, but rather, to attain to a state of unknowing. Upon this aspect of the mystical theology of St. John, R. J. Zwi Werblowsky remarks (1965:179–180),

As a mystic he *could* not possibly be a heretic, that is, by definition, one who holds deviant opinions, because it is not the mystic's business either to formulate or to defend theological opinions. His business is the emptying of the soul of all discursive contents.

Thus, there is the suggestion in St. John of the Cross that content-filled mystical states need to be rejected and this rejection is based upon the attainment of a state empty of all discursive contents, that is, a state of contentlessness. To be sure, this rejection of content-filled mystical states may be related to the fact that St. John was influenced by the Rhenish mystics and the Neo-platonic tradition as mediated through Pseudo-Dionysius in particular. But, if such influence is present, then this supports the notion that

St. John is a mystic who has attained contentless states, for, as indicated above, the Neo-platonic tradition is conducive to such attainment.

This point leads us to our fourth hypothesis, namely, that the pure mystical experience is most often attained in the context of an appropriate set of doctrines. Thus, one would not perhaps expect to find the 'pure' state as evident in those traditions in which there is, so to say, a teaching of the total discontinuity between man and God, and the world and God. We must be wary here of overstating the case, for, during the course of this study, we have examined a variety of passages within theistic contexts which appear to reflect the attainment of a state of contentlessness. Nevertheless, the predominant emphasis in the theistic traditions, and here one is thinking especially of Judaism, Christianity, and Islam, is that man only comes into relationship with the deity when the deity turns to man and reveals himself to him. We have suggested earlier in this study that the crucial means of the bridging of this gap between God and man may be seen as the theistic experience, exemplified in the experiences of such as Isaiah, Mohammed, and Moses and transmitted through the Scriptures, through worship, prayer, devotion, sacrifice, etc. Thus, it may at least be said that what the mystic does and says is not something which directs these traditions, but rather needs to be accommodated by them, or indeed, in some cases, rejected by them.

By contrast, within those traditions in which the mystic is the normative figure, the doctrines of which are reinforced by, if not ultimately dependent upon mystical experience, it is to be expected that the mystical experience will here reach its zenith. We have suggested that this zenith is the attainment of the contentlessness state and that this is that state attained pre-eminently in Buddhism, in Sānkhya-Yoga, and, one might add, in Advaita Vedānta and in the mysticism of Plotinus.

9

Conclusion

By way of conclusion, I want to sketch in outline the sort of conceptual framework for the study of mysticism that is implied by our discussion in the last few chapters. And in addition, I shall attempt to draw the threads of our discussion of the problem of conflicting truth claims together in the light of the conceptual framework thus outlined.

In the course of the last several chapters, we have been broadly concerned with the relationship between mystical experience and its interpretation. More specifically, we have examined a number of models of this relationship which have been proposed and used in a number of studies of mysticism. And we have noticed too, most significantly, that in a number of empirical accounts of specific mystical systems, one (or more) of these models has been implicitly and therefore uncritically assumed. I have argued that the first four of these models fail by relying on too crude a notion of the relationship between experience and interpretation. And my major contention has been that those accounts of mystical experience which are derived from the explicit or implicit use of such models are not acceptable because they are the result of inadequate methodological assumptions of the relationship of mystical experience and its interpretation.

In contrast to these, the view that there are as many types of mystical experience as there are incorporated interpretations of them circumvents a number of problems inherent in the alternative models. For it enabled us to make distinctions between interpretations which occur before, during, and after the mystical experience, thus allowing a more complete picture of the connections between the mystical experience, its cultural milieu, and retrospective interpretations of it to emerge.

Still, a doctrinaire application of this model is to be avoided. For we have to reckon with the possibility that mystical experiences may transcend their cultural contexts. And, as we have seen, there is the possibility that mystical experiences may so transcend by virtue of their contentlessness. Thus, as the nature of mystical experiences cannot be read solely from their retrospective interpretations, neither can they be read solely from their supposed incorporated interpretations. Reflexive interpretation does not *necessarily* reflect incorporated interpretation.

Such, in outline, is the conceptual framework for the study of mysticism which is implied by this study. Negatively, it means that, on the one hand, studies of mysticism which proceed solely from retrospective interpretations are inadequate; and that, on the other, those which extrapolate solely from the cultural and conceptual context in which mystical experiences occur are also inadequate. More positively, it means that the study of mysticism demands an engagement with the three inter-connected factors which we have separated, namely, the retrospective interpretation, the incorporated interpretation, and the experience itself.

In the course of this study, a number of points have been made regarding the appropriate way in which to analyse retrospective interpretations — the necessity of distinguishing between first, second, and third order categories of interpretation and between different levels of mystical experience, the place of the notion of ineffability in mystical language, the use by mystics of sacred texts, the question of the experiential base of mystical texts, and so on. But a further point of particular importance may be added to these in the light of the role which incorporated interpretation may play in any mystical experience. This is to the effect that where there is a substantial difference between a retrospective interpretation of mystical experience and the interpretation which one might have expected to be incorporated into the experience as a result of the mystic's context, then it is possible, even probable, that the experience has transcended its context, and that the retrospective interpretation more closely reflects the nature of the experience. In other words, in a case of this sort, the crucial factor in the conflict between the retrospective and incorporated interpretations is the experience itself.

But this too reinforces the necessity for any study of mysticism to be contextually based. Model five implies that the major formative factor of mystical experience is the context in which it occurs. The mystical experience is *crucially* (although not *necessarily*) context dependent. A sociological, anthropological, and historical approach to particular mystical systems is consequently necessary if the mystical endeavour is to be placed within the societal and cultural framework as a whole. It is only in the recognition of the interplay between retrospective and incorporated interpretations within specific cultural contexts that we may hope to generate accurate accounts of the mystical experiences that arise out of them.

A further major conclusion relates to the above point. The recognition of the crucial role played by incorporated interpretation in mystical experiences entails the development of a much more complex phenomenology of mystical experience. A much richer and more complete picture of the nature of mystical experience comes into view.

This more complex phenomenology of mystical experience implies too a much more complex pattern of relationships between mystical experience and religious doctrines. For on the one hand, we have recognized that doctrines may shape the nature of the experience itself through being incorporated into it. Yet, on the other hand, because mystical experience may go beyond its incorporated content, we have to reckon with the possibility that such experiences may be decisive in the formulation or revision of doctrinal frameworks, and that they may provide the impetus also for important changes in the societal and cultural framework as a whole. This more complex relationship between mystical experiences and religious doctrines has consequences as well for the attempt to resolve conflicting religious truth claims by appeal to mystical experience. And it is important therefore to consider this question again in the light of our discussion in the second part of this book.

According to the results of our study, any formulation of the relationship between religious experience and religious expression must take into consideration the various forms of religious experience which we have attempted to isolate and delineate, namely, theistic experiences, the varieties of content-filled mystical experiences (including theistic mystical experiences), and the 'pure' contentless mystical experience. To this extent therefore, the question of the resolution of conflicting truth claims is immeasurably more complex than is evident in the analyses of those writers examined earlier in this study. Thus, Radhakrishnan's and Stace's resolutions are based only upon the 'pure' experience; Zaehner's normative resolution does not take into account the phenomenology of the theistic experience, nor the large variety of content-filled mystical experiences, even within what might be loosely called 'theistically-oriented' mystical experiences; Otto's Friesian presuppositions lead him to a neglect of the phenomenological differences between theistic experience and the 'pure' contentless state; and finally, although Smart appears to recognize the possibility of content-filled mystical states, his attempted resolution proceeds upon the basis of the determining of the correct synthesis of theistic and 'pure' contentless experiences. Thus, if a resolution were possible, it would need to take into consideration the much more complex phenomenology of religious experience implied by the theoretical framework developed in the latter part of this study.

But further, there is a sense in which the results which have accrued not only indicate the complexity of the actual task, but also raise the question of its conceptual possibility. In order to illuminate this, let us leave theistic experience out of consideration for the moment, and concentrate on the mystical experience.

The attempt to resolve conflicting truth claims, or more generally to determine religious truth, by an appeal to the nature of mystical experience appears to be a conceptually possible task if two presuppositions are made: Firstly, that all interpretations of mystical experience occur retrospectively; secondly, and following from this, that there is a unanimity of mystical experience which can be discerned if only one can clear away the overlaid subsequent interpretations. Thus, operating on these two presuppositions, it appears to be possible, through the determination of the nature of mystical experience, then to ascertain those doctrines which most closely reflect it.

This study has brought into question both of these presuppositions. It has been maintained that, because interpretations are incorporated into mystical experiences, there are varieties of them. And consequently, the appeal to a universal core of mystical experience as a means of resolving the problem of conflicting religious truth claims is ruled out of court. Moreover, if paradigmatic expressions are incorporated into mystical experience, it is viciously circular to appeal to these experiences in support of the truth of the thus-incorporated doctrines.

A further implication deserves mentioning. Because the nature of mystical experience is determined to a crucial extent by what is incorporated into it, the truth of the content of the experiences becomes the question of the truth of the doctrines which are thus incorporated. Thus, the conceptual framework which we have developed in this study implies that the attempt to reconcile conflicting truth claims between different religions by appeal to mystical experience is nugatory. And this suggests that the attempt to resolve the problem needs to be conducted on extra-experiential grounds.

To be sure, I have been at pains to point out that mystical experiences may transcend their cultural contexts, and that in the case of contentless experiences no incorporated interpretation at all is present during them. On the face of it, it may appear that I have suggested that the core of mystical experience is the pure contentless state and that, therefore, those doctrines which reflect it may be more true because more reflective of that state. However, the term 'pure' has been intended only in a phenomenological sense, and not in an evaluative one. But even if 'pure' were intended in an evaluative way, and it was argued that the most true mystical doctrines were those conducive to and reflective of the contentless experience, this would still fail to bring a decisive resolution of the problem of conflicting religious truth claims. For, as I have suggested, the contentless experience may occur in

Theravāda Buddhism, in Sānkhya-Yoga, in Advaita Vedānta, and in the mysticism of Plotinus. The contentless experience is compatible with a number of conflicting doctrinal systems, and herein lies its appeal for those who, like Radhakrishnan, argue for the thesis of the unity of all religions by appeal to it. Again, only extra-experiential criteria could resolve the problem of conflicting religious truth claims in religious systems grounded in a common experience that transcends their respective contexts.

In sum therefore, as a result of the conceptual framework proposed in this study, the attempt to resolve the problem of conflicting religious truth claims by appeal to mystical experience is fraught with difficulties, both conceptually and in practice. Indeed, the overall thrust of our argument suggests that, whether we are concerned with content-filled mystical experiences, or with the limiting case of contentless mystical experiences, the resolution of the problem of conflicting religious truth claims devolves on the establishment of extra-experiential criteria.

In the final analysis, this study has been a programmatic one. For it is to be hoped that the conceptual framework developed will lead to a clearer appreciation of the nature of mystical experience, to a more finely-tuned awareness of its complex relation to the structure of religious formulations, to contextually rich studies of various mystical traditions, and finally to further attempts to refine the criteria necessary for the resolution of conflicting religious truth claims. It is to be hoped that this study has moved some little way towards the realization of these goals.

NOTES TO CHAPTER TWO

1. And also with reference to that group of Islamic perennialists whose mode of thought is exemplified in the writings of F. Schuon, R. Guenon, and S. H. Nasr. See, for example, Needleman 1974, and Schuon 1976.

2. Zaehner's category of panenhenic experience is closely related to that which R. M. Bucke takes to be the essence of the mystical experience, namely, 'cosmic consciousness'. See Bucke 1966:17–18. Bucke maintains that cosmic consciousness 'shows the cosmos to consist not of dead matter governed by unconscious, rigid and unintending laws; it shows it on the contrary as entirely immaterial, entirely spiritual and entirely alive; it shows that death is an absurdity, that everything and everyone has eternal life; it shows that the Universe is God and that God is the Universe, and that no evil ever did or ever will enter into it'. See also Zaehner 1970:40–60.

3. In *Concordant Discord*, the category of panenhenic experience is further divided into the components of 'transcending of spatial limitations' and 'transcending of temporal limitations'. Thus, four types of mystical experience are distinguished. The expanded classification does not affect our analysis at this point.

4. The context is that of Krishna justifying in a fairly crude way to Arjuna the killing of the latter's relatives in the battle about to commence. Arjuna's trepidations are to be mollified by the realization that only the body and not the soul is slain.

5. The passage, dealing as it does with rebirth, appears to have no relation of content to panenhenic experience. The eternity of the *soul*, if this bears any relationship to mystical experience, would relate more suitably to Zaehner's monistic category.

6. I believe that Zaehner overstates the case with regard to the meaning of 'māya' as in the following passage from *Mysticism Sacred and Profane*, p. 156:
'Once release is achieved, it is realized that since nothing exists except the One, realized as oneself, all actions, all religious ceremonies, all devotion addressed to any God, the Gods, or God himself are pure illusion and absolute nothingness.' Thus, I prefer to take 'māyā' as the 'not-having of ontological ultimacy'. For the enlightened man, the realm of manifest reality has no ultimacy.

7. Thus in *Mysticism Sacred and Profane*, we have three varieties; in *Concordant Discord*, we have four varieties with the first two converging into the third; in *Zen, Drugs and Mysticism* (1972), we have four varieties with a clear distinction between the first two and the third; and in 'Mysticism Without Love', we have the original three varieties. The category of theistic mystical experience remains constant throughout.

8. With respect to the *Gītā* (at least), there is of course the prior question whether it *does* assert that the theistic mystical experience *is* a higher state. Since this is a question of literary exegesis without immediate philosophical ramifications, I shall not take it further.

9. There are, of course, sound Upanishadic reasons for such a stance. See, for example, *Brihadāranyaka* Upanishad 1.4.10.

10. In correspondence with me on a related issue, Professor James Horne drew my attention to a passage in Martin Buber's *Between Man and Man* in which Buber appears to cite his own transcending of monistic experience for the higher reality of

'self in relation to others', and 'self in relation to God'. The issue of Buber's mysticism is a complex one. But Buber certainly does not appear to be arguing that the I-divine Thou relation is a form of theistic mystical experience (in Zaehner's sense).

11.   It is also worth noting that with reference to al-Ghazālī, Zaehner states quite clearly in *Hindu and Muslim Mysticism* (1969:166) that al-Ghazālī adopts a theistic stance only for apologetic reasons. Thus, of al-Ghazālī's Persian commentary on the *Mishkat*, namely, Fadā'il al-Anām, Zaehner remarks, 'Here at last Ghazālī forgets to worry about the orthodoxy he usually chooses to parade, and declares himself a non-dualist of whom Śankara himself might have been proud'.

NOTES TO CHAPTER THREE

1.   For a more detailed discussion of this point in Otto, see Chapter five of this volume. For an example of this technique in Wach, see esp. J. Wach, 'The Study of Mahāyāna Buddhism', in Wach 1951.

2.   The distinction between the forms of expression and these two types of religious experience was, to my knowledge, first made by Nathan Söderblom. The most lucid adumbration in English is to be found in Hastings's *Encyclopaedia of Religion and Ethics*, vol. 3, p. 738.

3.   That experience of Tennyson's arising from his repeating his own name to himself is slightly different. Such repetition has parallels to the use of *mantras* in the Indian tradition and the 'Jesus Prayer' in the Hesychast tradition of Eastern Orthodox Christianity. It may also be noted that, while there is a certain measure of spontaneity to such experiences, in the cases of Reid, Joel, and Jefferies, certain physical conditions nonetheless conduce towards the occurrence of such experiences.

4.   In fact, within this passage are two quite different notions of the relation between experience and interpretation. Smart, however, develops his critique of Zaehner on the basis of interpretation as retrospective to experience.

5.   Perhaps the major exponent of the view that the Buddha taught a soul doctrine is Margaret Rhys Davids. According to her, the teaching of the Buddha was in accord with the Upanishadic doctrine of the immanent *ātman*. For a critique of her position see Murti 1960:20–24.

6.   For a more extended critique, see Smart 1964a:211–213. The issue at stake is an important one, and therefore a few words of comment may be fruitful. Thus, there can firstly be no doubt that there are many texts which imply the doctrine of *anatta*. These may take any of three forms. Firstly, there are those which deny that there is anything in the physical or mental realms which may properly be called one's self for in these realms impermanence and dependence rule. This is not the denial of the 'self' as such, but only the denial of the possibility of its identity with anything in the phenomenal realm. Secondly, there are those texts which conceive of man as *only* an aggregate of causally-connected psychic and physical elements. Here, there is quite explicit denial of the 'self'. Thirdly, there are those texts which support a middle position between *atta* and *anatta*. I would want to suggest that this middle position is most probably that of the Buddha himself. And further, I would agree with T. R. V. Murti, G. C. Pande (1957:504–510), and S. Radhakrishnan (1958, I, 682–683) that the correct interpretation of the Buddha's silence (for example, in S. N. 44.X.10) is that the true state of affairs is beyond words and thought.

7.   Although, as indicated in the previous note, the Buddha does not admit to a certain connection between *'anatta'* and mystical experience, this should not be taken as an indication that, in so far as mystical experience is conceptualized, a better case cannot

be made out for *anatta* as a more correct interpretation of the mystical experience than *atta*. In spite of this, the silence of the Buddha on the question still places Zaehner on the horns of a dilemma.

8. On the nature and function of the gods in Theravāda Buddhism, see von Glasenapp 1970, chs. 1 and 2.

9. Smart also refers to the *Mishkāt* of Al-Ghazālī, specifically the passage quoted at the end of the last chapter, as further evidence for his thesis.

10. This passage appears in a context in which the distinction between monistic and theistic mystical experience is allied with a theological excursus on the fall of man.

11. Similar criteria are adduced by James Horne (1975:288) in his attempt to distinguish true and false mystics in 'Which Mystic Has The Revelation?' According to Horne, the mystic who should be believed, '. . . ideally exhibits a character of integrity, accomplishment, and deep rooted sanity, and he incorporates in his statements and expands upon, the religious knowledge already enunciated in a viable religious community'. Horne, like Zaehner, fails to distinguish between criteria which are utilized within religious communities, and criteria which can be validated independently of specific religious communities. To this extent, Horne's criteria come under similar criticism to those of Zaehner.

12. For reasons that will become clear in Chapter 5 of this study, I shall substitute the term 'theistic experience' for Smart's term 'numinous experience'.

13. Otto, in spite of his Kantian framework derived from Jakob Fries, stands firmly within Schleiermacher's critique of the Kantian account of religion. For example, see Otto's Introduction to Schleiermacher 1958:xix.

14. Otto is very much heir to the nineteenth-century approach to *Religionsgeschichte*. This was dominated by the quest for the origins of religion, and therefore, the postulation of the evolutionary development of religion was very much in evidence.

15. Smart writes: 'It is worth commenting too on the way in which the religion of worship is expressed by the notion of and distinction between the Lord and selves. For the attitude of worship, and a sense of the holy or numinous other, as Object of worship, implies a distinction between the worshipper and the Object of worship'.

NOTES TO CHAPTER FOUR

1. The passages drawn from Eckhart are derived from Otto's analysis of the mysticism of Eckhart and Shankara. As far as I have been able, I have checked the passages quoted against available translations of Eckhart's writings. I can find there also no autobiographical statements making the connection of panenhenic expression and panenhenic experience explicit.

2. It is interesting to note that Stace omits the word 'inwardly' from the quotation from Underhill. I have inserted it in square brackets in the text.

3. For a number of characterizations of alternative meanings of 'subjectivity', 'objectivity', and so on, see W. J. Wainwright 1970:143–144.

4. I am, of course, not supporting the case for soul pluralism, but merely indicating a possible Sānkhyin perspective on Stace's claims.

5. Stace fails to make a clear distinction between mind and soul, a distinction of some importance and subtlety in Sānkhya. See Dasgupta 1973:17–23.

6. The paradox remains in the *Bhagavad-Gītā*; compare chs. 11 and 13. 12–17. The paradox is, in many cases however, resolved: In Shankara, by means of the distinction between *saguna* and *nirguna* Brahman; in Mahāyāna, by means of the doctrine of the *trikāya*, see Suzuki 1963:243–276; in Eastern Orthodoxy, through the distinction between the essence (*ousia*) of God and his relation to created being (*oikonomia*),

see Lossky 1957, ch. 4; and in Eckhart, dependent especially upon the Pseudo-Dionysian teaching on the God of unknowing, by means of the notion of the Godhead beyond the triune deity, see Schürmann 1978:114–121.

7. Speaking of the 'six systems' of Indian philosophy, Joseph Campbell remarks that they 'never attained the position of an exclusive dogmatic orthodoxy'. 'In the final analysis', he continues, 'the orthodoxy of India has never been grounded in a college or academy. Neither can it be defined by any numbering of views. For its life is in the *mokṣa* of the actual sages'. See appendices by Campbell in Zimmer 1956:613–614.

8. God, in Madhva's system, has quite explicitly positive qualities. S. N. Dasgupta (1969, IV, 155) remarks, 'God, or Paramātman, is in this system [i.e. Madhva's] considered as the fulness of infinite qualities. He is the author of creation, maintenance, destruction, control, knowledge, bondage, salvation, and hiding . . .'

9. This is not to maintain that the world as *perceived* is real, for this would be incompatible with the concept of *anicca* (impermanence). As Murti (1960:73) notes, 'The real is momentary; it is particular, unique . . . Existence is the momentary flash into being . . .'

10. Suso says, 'For it [the spirit] receives indeed some attributes of Godhead, but it does not become God by nature . . . It is still a something which has been created out of nothing and continues to be this everlastingly.'

11. It is true that in Plotinian union there is no longer consciousness of difference from the One, no longer Seer and Seen, but only unity. Yet, there is never any suggestion in Plotinus that all things except the One are merely fleeting appearances. Platonic 'realism' runs too deep for this.

NOTES TO CHAPTER FIVE

1. The logic of the assumption to which Underhill refers is well spelt out with reference to the Indian tradition in Varenne 1976:45.

2. For early examples of the Absolutist tendency in Indian thought, see *Rig Veda* 1.164.6 and 1.164.46. There has been much debate on the historical influence of Indian thought upon Neo-platonic absolutism. The most notable proponent of the argument for such a connection is E. Brehier, *The Philosophy of Plotinus* (1959). For a critique of his position, see Armstrong 1936:22–38.

3. For a modern example of this thrust towards Being, see Tillich 1951, I, 189 and 1962: 34, 40, 43, 48. A most notable modern exception to this rule is Martin Heidegger. For an interesting argument on similarities between Heidegger and Buddhism see Steffney 1977.

4. The crucial factor in this mode of thought may well be Nāgārjuna's assertion of the sameness of Nirvāna and Samsāra. See Nāgārjuna's *Mūlamadhyamaka kārika*, 25.

5. The most accessible source of Fries's philosophy in German is his popular summary *Wissen, Glaube und Ahndung* (1931). The best account in English is R. Otto, *The Philosophy of Religion* (1931). A useful summary may be found in R. F. Davidson 1947, and Bastow 1976.

6. Fries's notion of *'Ahnung'* is quite clearly related to Schleiermacher's claim that the essence of religion is 'intuition' and 'feeling' (*Anschauung* and *Gefühl*) for the Eternal in the temporal and the Infinite in the finite. See especially Schleiermacher 1958:275–284.

7. Otto's belief that Fries has overcome the subjectivism of Kant invalidates H. J. Paton's claim that Otto is unaware of the difficulty inherent in basing religious knowledge on Kantian subjectivism. In fact, Paton seems to be unaware himself of the relation of Otto to Fries for he makes no reference to the latter. See Paton 1955:129–145.

8. But see also p. 3 where Otto criticizes Christianity for failing to recognize the value of the non-rational element in religion, thus giving to the idea of God a one-sidedly intellectualistic and rationalistic interpretation.

NOTES TO CHAPTER SEVEN

1. Although not immediately pertinent to our concerns at this moment, it is worth noting that both James and Stace fail to distinguish between the ineffability of the experience and the mystical doctrine of the ineffability of the 'object' of mystical experience.
2. S. N. Dasgupta's classification parallels Larson's closely too; see *Hindu Mysticism* (1927).
3. Fakhry argues that the neo-Aristotelian Alexander of Aphrodisias (c.205 A.D.) is not the source of this mysticism; cf. Merlan 1963: 18ff. A. Altmann (1969:103–104; and Enneads, VI.9.8), while recognizing Alexander as a possible source, argues for Plotinus as the most likely source of this form of mysticism.
4. Although Fakhry (1971:207) ventures it as a possibility that the differences in paradigmatic expression between visionary and unitary mysticism may be due to the influences of the Islamic doctrinal scheme and not to the varying content of the mystical experience.
5. I am indebted to P. G. Moore (1978:103) for this distinction. Moore's distinction between third order reports and the other two categories is somewhat parallel to B. K. Matilal's (1975:217–252) between reports of the ineffability of the object and ineffability of the experience. 'First order accounts' is analogous to our earlier enunciated autobiographical principle.
6. Although Moore offers no examples of radical ineffability in third-order statements, the following references would be representative: Gregory Nazianzus, *The Second Theological Oration*, in H. Ware and P. Schaff (1894, vol. 7, p. 294); *Tao te Ching*, ch. 1 and Waley (1958:142–143); Pseudo-Dionysius, *The Mystical Theology*, ch. 5; *Enneads*, 5.3.13 and Rist (1964:69–70). The limiting case of radical ineffability is the Mādhyamika school of the Mahāyāna.
7. With respect to the Incarnation, however, I think it could be argued plausibly that it is the union of the divine and human in Christ which fore-shadows the interpretation of mystical union as the co-mingling of the divine and the human (see, for example, Lossky 1957:10).

NOTES TO CHAPTER EIGHT

1. 'Contact with the One' is one of Plotinus' favourite metaphors for mystical union with the One. See, for example, *Enneads*, 6.9.11; cf. also Rist 1967:198.
2. I have avoided the problem of the relationship of the attainment of the *jhānas* to the attainment of *Nirvāna*. There is a tradition of interpretation of the Pali canon that *Nirvāna* can be attained at any point along the path of contemplation, or even before beginning upon it.

References

Abe, M. (1975). Non-Being and *Mu*: The Metaphysical Nature of Negativity in the East and the West. *Religious Studies* 11, 181–92.

Almond, P. C. (1977). Review of D. Z. Phillips (1976). *Australasian Journal of Philosophy* 55, 218–221.

— (1981). A Note on Theologizing about Religions. *The Journal of Theological Studies*, 32, 178–180.

Altmann, A. (1969). *Studies in Religious Philosophy and Mysticism*. London: Routledge and Kegan Paul.

Arberry, A. J. (1950). *Sufism*. London: Allen and Unwin.

Armstrong, A. H. (1936). Plotinus and India. *Classical Quarterly* 30, 22–38.

— (1967). Plotinus. In *The Cambridge History of Later Greek and Early Medieval Philosophy*, A. H. Armstrong (ed.), 193–268. Cambridge: Cambridge University Press.

Ayer, A. J. (1970). *Language, Truth and Logic*. London: Gollancz.

Bastow, D. (1976). Otto and Numinous Experience. *Religious Studies* 12, 159–176.

Benz, E. (1965). *Buddhism or Communism*. London: Allen and Unwin.

Blakney, R. B. (ed.) (1941). *Meister Eckhart*. New York: Harper and Row.

Blofeld, J. (1970). *The Way of Power*. London: Allen and Unwin.

Braithwaite, R. B. (1971). An Empiricist's View of the Nature of Religious Belief. In *The Philosophy of Religion*, B. Mitchell (ed.), 72–91. London: Oxford University Press.

Brehier, E. (1959). *The Philosophy of Plotinus*. Chicago: University of Chicago Press.

Buber, M. (1961). *Between Man and Man*. London: Collins.

Bucke, R. M. (1966). *Cosmic Consciousness*. New York: E. P. Dutton.

Buddhaghosa (1971). *Visuddhimagga*, trans. by Pe Maung Tin. London: Luzac and Company.

Butler, C. (1967). *Western Mysticism*. London: Constable.

Capitan, W. H. and Merrill, D. D. (eds.) (1965). *Art, Mind and Religion*. Pennsylvania: University of Pittsburgh Press.

Christian, W. A. (1972). *Opposition of Religious Doctrines*. London: Macmillan.

Collins, J. B. (1971). *Christian Mysticism in the Elizabethan Age*. New York: Octagon Books.

Copleston, F. C. (1976). Hegel and the Rationalization of Mysticism. In *Philosophers and Philosophies*, F. C. Copleston. London: Search Press.

Corbin, H. (1969). *Creative Imagination in the Sufism of Ibn 'Arabī*. Princeton: Princeton University Press.

Coward, H. and Penelhum, T. (1977). *Mystics and Scholars*. Ontario: Wilfrid Laurier University Press.

Dasgupta, S. N. (1927). *Hindu Mysticism*. New York: Ungar.

— (1969). *A History of Indian Philosophy*. Cambridge: Cambridge University Press.

— (1973). *Yoga as Philosophy and Religion*. Delhi: Motilal Barnasidass.

Davidson, R. F. (1947). *Rudolf Otto's Interpretation of Religion*. Princeton: Princeton University Press.

Deussen, P. (1973). *The System of the Vedānta*. New York: Dover.

Dodds, E. R. (1960). Tradition and Personal Achievement in the Philosophy of Plotinus. *Journal of Roman Studies* 50, 1–7.

— (1965). *Pagan and Christian in an Age of Anxiety*. Cambridge: Cambridge University Press.

Edgerton, F. (1924). The Meaning of Sānkhya and Yoga. *American Journal of Philology* 45, 1-26.

Eliade, M. (1965). *The Two and the One*. London: Harvihill.

Fakhry, M. (1970). *A History of Islamic Philosophy*. New York: Columbia University Press.

— (1971). Three Varieties of Mysticism in Islam. *International Journal for the Philosophy of Religion* 2, 193-207.

Fries, J. (1931). *Wissen, Glaube und Ahndung*. Göttingen: Öffentliches Leben Verlag.

Garside, B. (1972). Language and the Interpretation of Mystical Experience. *International Journal for the Philosophy of Religion* 3, 93-102.

Gibbs, B. (1976). Mysticism and the Soul. *Monist* 59, 532-549.

Gimello, R. M. (1978). Mysticism and Meditation. In *Mysticism and Philosophical Analysis*, S. Katz (ed.), 170-199. London: Sheldon Press.

von Glasenapp, H. (1970). *Buddhism, a Non-Theistic Religion*. London: Allen and Unwin.

Gowen, J. (1973). Religion, Reason and Ninian Smart. *Religious Studies* 9, 219-227.

Griffiths, B. (1978). *Return to the Centre*. London: Fount.

Happold, F. C. (1970). *Mysticism*. Harmondsworth: Penguin.

Hawi, S. S. (1974). *Islamic Naturalism and Mysticism*. Leiden: Brill.

Hepburn, R. W. (1958). *Christianity and Paradox*. London: Watts.

— (1971). From World to God. In *The Philosophy of Religion*, B. Mitchell (ed.), 168-178. London: Oxford University Press.

Hick, J. (ed.) (1974a). *Truth and Dialogue*. London: Sheldon Press.

— (1974b). The Outcome: Dialogue into Truth. In J. Hick (ed.) (1974a), 140-155.

— (1977a). *God and the Universe of Faiths*. London: Fount.

— (1977b). Mystical Experience as Cognition. In *Mystics and Scholars*, H. Coward and T. Penelhum (eds.), 41-56. Ontario: Wilfrid Laurier University Press.

— (1980). *God Has Many Names*. London: Macmillan.

Hick, J. and Hebblethwaite, B. (eds.) (1980). *Christianity and Other Religions*. London: Fount.

Hiriyanna, M. (1932). *Outlines of Indian Philosophy*. London: Allen and Unwin.

Horne, J. (1975). Which Mystic has the Revelation? *Religious Studies* 11, 283-291.

Inge, W. R. (1969). *Mysticism in Religion*. London: Rider and Co.

James, W. (1961). *The Varieties of Religious Experience*. London: Collins.

Johansson, R. (1969). *The Psychology of Nirvana*. London: Allen and Unwin.

Johnston, W. J. (1977). *Silent Music*. London: Fount.

— (1978). *The Inner Eye of Love*. London: Collins.

Jones, R. M. (1909). *Studies in Mystical Religion*. London: Macmillan.

Jung, C. G. (1919). *Psychology of the Unconscious*. London: Routledge and Kegan Paul.

Katz, S. T. (1978). Language, Epistemology and Mysticism. In *Mysticism and Philosophical Analysis*, S. T. Katz (ed.), 22-74. London: Sheldon Press.

Kennick, W. E. (1962). Review of W. T. Stace (1961). *The Philosophical Review* 71, 387-390.

Kierkegaard, S. (1936). *Philosophical Fragments*. Princeton: Princeton University Press.

Kraemer, H. (1950). *World Cultures and World Religions: The Coming Dialogue*. Philadelphia: Westminster Press.

— (1956). *Religion and the Christian Faith*. London: Lutterworth.

Küng, H. (1967). The World's Religions in God's Plan of Salvation. In *Christian Revelation and World Religions*, J. Neuner (ed.). London: Burns and Oates.

Larson, G. J. (1969). *Classical Sāmkhya*. Delhi: Motilal Barnasidass.

— (1973). Mystical Man in India. *Journal for the Scientific Study of Religion* 12, 1-16.

Laski, M. (1961). *Ecstasy*. London: Cresset.

Ling, T. (1961). *Buddha, Marx and God*. London: Macmillan.
— (1965). Buddhist Mysticism. *Religious Studies* 1, 163–175.
Lossky, V. (1957). *The Mystical Theology of the Eastern Church*. Cambridge: Clarke and Co.
Martin, C. B. (1959). *Religious Belief*. Ithaca: Cornell University Press.
Masters, R. E. L. and Houston, J. (1966). *The Varieties of Psychedelic Experience*. New York: Delta.
Matilal, B. K. (1975). Mysticism and Reality: Ineffability. *Journal of Indian Philosophy* 3, 217–252.
Merlan, Ph. (1963). *Monopsychism, Mysticism, Metaconsciousness*. Leiden: Brill.
Merton, T. (1961). *Mystics and Zen Masters*. New York: Delta.
Moffitt, J. (1973). *Journey to Gorakhpur*. London: Sheldon Press.
Moore, J. M. (1938). *Theories of Religious Experience*. New York: Round Table Press.
Moore, P. G. (1973). Recent Studies of Mysticism. *Religion* 3, 146–156.
— (1978). Mystical Experience, Mystical Doctrine, Mystical Technique. In *Mysticism and Philosophical Analysis*, S. T. Katz (ed.), 101–131. London: Sheldon Press.
Mortley, R. (1975). Negative Theology and Abstraction in Plotinus. *American Journal of Philology* 96, 363–377.
Murti, T. R. V. (1960). *The Central Philosophy of Buddhism*. London: Allen and Unwin.
Needleman, J. (ed.) (1974). *The Sword of Gnosis*. Baltimore: Penguin.
Neuner, J. (ed.) (1967). *Christian Revelation and World Religions*. London: Burns and Oates.
Nicholson, R. A. (1963). *The Mystics of Islam*. London: Routledge and Kegan Paul.
Otto, R. (1931). *The Philosophy of Religion*. London: Norgate and Williams.
— (1932). *Mysticism East and West*. New York: Macmillan.
— (1958). *The Idea of the Holy*. London: Oxford University Press.
van Over, R. *Chinese Mystics*. New York: Harper and Row.
Owen, H. P. (1971). Christian Mysticism. *Religious Studies* 7, 31–42.
Pande, G. C. (1957). *Studies in the Origin of Buddhism*. Allahabad: University of Allahabad Press.
Pannikar, K. M. (1969). *Asia and Western Dominance*. New York: Collier.
Parkinson, G. H. R. (1977). Hegel, Pantheism, and Spinoza. *Journal of the History of Ideas* 38, 449–459.
Parrinder, G. (1976). *Mysticism in the World's Religions*. London: Sheldon Press.
Paton, H. J. (1955). *The Modern Predicament*. London: Allen and Unwin.
Peers, E. Allison (1960). *The Life of St. Teresa of Jesus*. New York: Image Books.
Penelhum, T. (1977). Unity and Diversity in the Interpretation of Mysticism. In *Mystics and Scholars*, T. Penelhum and H. Coward (eds.), 71–81. Ontario: Wilfrid Laurier University Press.
Phillips, D. Z. (1976). *Religion Without Explanation*. London: Blackwell.
Pike, N. (1965). Comments. In *Art, Mind and Religion*, W. H. Capitan and D. D. Merrill (eds.), 144–150. Pennsylvania: University of Pittsburgh Press.
Pletcher, G. K. (1972). Agreement Among Mystics. *Sophia* 11(2), 5–15.
Radhakrishnan, S. (1933). *East and West in Religion*. London: Allen and Unwin.
— (1940). *Eastern Religions and Western Thought*. London: Oxford University Press.
— (1953). *The Principal Upaniṣads*. London: Allen and Unwin.
— (1958). *Indian Philosophy*. London: Allen and Unwin.
— (1975). *The Hindu View of Life*. New York: Macmillan.
Reid, Forrest (1902). *Following Darkness*. London: Arnold.
Richards, G. (1980). Towards a Theology of Religions. *The Journal of Theological Studies* 31, 44–66.

Rist, J. M. (1964). *Eros and Psyche*. Toronto: University of Toronto Press.
— (1967). *The Road to Reality*. Cambridge: University of Cambridge Press.
van Ruysbroeck, Jan (1952). *The Spiritual Espousals*. London: Faber and Faber.
Schimmel, A. (1975). *Mystical Dimensions of Islam*. Chapel Hill: The University of North Carolina Press.
Schleiermacher, F. (1948). *The Christian Faith*. Edinburgh: T. and T. Clark.
— (1958). *On Religion: Speeches to its Cultured Despisers*. New York: Harper and Row.
Scholem, G. G. (1961). *Major Trends in Jewish Mysticism*. New York: Schocken.
— (1965). *On the Kabbalah and its Symbolism*. New York: Schocken.
Schürmann, R. (1978). *Meister Eckhart: Mystic and Philosopher*. Bloomington: Indiana University Press.
Schuon, F. (1976). *Islam and the Perennial Philosophy*. U.K.: World of Islam Publishing Company.
Sherrard, P. (1974). The Tradition and the Traditions. *Religious Studies* 10, 407–17.
Smart, N. (1958). *Reasons and Faiths*. London: Routledge and Kegan Paul.
— (1962). Mystical Experience. *Sophia* 1(1), 19–26.
— (1964a). *Doctrine and Argument in Indian Philosophy*. London: Allen and Unwin.
— (1964b). *Philosophers and Religious Truth*. London: S.C.M. Press.
— (1965a). Interpretation and Mystical Experience. *Religious Studies* 1, 75–87.
— (1965b). Rejoinders. In *Art, Mind and Religion*, W. H. Capitan and D. D. Merrill (eds.), 156–158. Pennsylvania: University of Pittsburgh Press.
— (1968). *The Yogi and the Devotee*. London: Allen and Unwin.
— (1971). *The Religious Experience of Mankind*. London: Fontana.
Smith, M. (1976). *The Way of the Mystics*. London: Sheldon Press.
— (1977). *An Introduction to Mysticism*. London: Sheldon Press.
Smith, W. Cantwell (1959). Comparative Religion: Whither — and Why? In *The History of Religions*, M. Eliade and J. M. Kitagawa (eds.), 31–58. Chicago: University of Chicago Press.
— (1967). *Questions of Religious Truth*. New York: Scribners.
Spencer, S. (1971). *Mysticism in World Religion*. Massachusetts: Peter Smith.
Staal, F. (1975). *Exploring Mysticism*. Harmondsworth: Penguin.
Stace, W. T. (1961). *Mysticism and Philosophy*. London: Macmillan.
Steffney, J. (1977). Transmetaphysical Thinking in Heidegger and Zen. *Philosophy East and West* 27, 323–333.
Streng, F. J. (1978). Language and Mystical Awareness. In *Mysticism and Philosophical Analysis*, S. Katz (ed.), 141–169. London: Sheldon Press.
Suzuki, D. T. (1957). *Mysticism Christian and Buddhist*. London: Allen and Unwin.
— (1960). *Manual of Zen Buddhism*. New York: Grove Press.
— (1963). *Outlines of Mahāyāna Buddhism*. New York: Schocken.
Tillich, P. (1951). *Systematic Theology*. Chicago: University of Chicago Press.
— (1962). *The Courage to Be*. London: Fontana.
— (1963). *Christianity and the Encounter of the World Religions*. New York: Columbia University Press.
Troeltsch, E. (1972). *The Absoluteness of Christianity*. London: S.C.M.
Underhill, E. (1930). *Mysticism*. London: Methuen.
— (1977). The Mysticism of Plotinus. *Journal of Studies in Mysticism* 1, 82–113.
Varenne, J. (1976). *Yoga and the Hindu Tradition*. Chicago: University of Chicago Press.
Wach, J. (1944). *Sociology of Religion*. Chicago: University of Chicago Press.
— (1951). *Types of Religious Experience*. Chicago: University of Chicago Press.
Wainwright, W. J. (1970). Stace and Mysticism. *Journal of Religion* 50, 139–154.
Waley, A. (1958). *The Way and its Power*. New York: Grove Press.
Wallis, R. T. (1972). *Neo-Platonism*. New York: Scribners.

Ware, H. and Schaff, P. (1894). *A Select Library of Nicene and Post-Nicene Fathers*. Oxford: Parker and Co.

Werblowsky, R. J. Zwi (1965). On the Mystical Rejection of Mystical Illuminations. *Religious Studies* 1, 177–184.

Wittgenstein, L. (1972). *Philosophical Investigations*. Oxford: Blackwell.

Wood, C. M. (1975). *Theory and Understanding*. Montana: Scholars Press.

Zaehner, R. C. (1961). *Mysticism, Sacred and Profane*. London: Oxford University Press.

— (1966). *Hinduism*. Oxford: Oxford University Press.

— (1969). *Hindu and Muslim Mysticism*. New York: Schocken.

— (1970). *Concordant Discord*. London: Oxford University Press.

— (1972). *Zen, Drugs and Mysticism*. New York: Vintage.

— (1974). Mysticism Without Love. *Religious Studies* 10, 257–264.

Zimmer, H. (1956). *Philosophies of India*. New York: Meridian.

Religions and Societies: Asia and the Middle East

Edited by Carlo Caldarola

1982. 14,8 x 22,8 cm. VIII, 688 pages.
Clothbound. DM 125,−; US $57.00   ISBN 90 279 3259 X
(Religion and Society 22)

From the preface by the Series Editors:

This kind of handbook on religion in Asia and the Middle East has three main goals. First it intends to provide an integrated and objective profile of the interaction of religions and societies in a number of countries of Asia and the Middle East. Second it is meant to encourage comparative and theoretical considerations by identifying not only certain patterns of interaction between religion and society in general but also those patterns which seem to be characteristic for each religion and can be studied through a variety of socio-cultural contexts. And third the book should provide, as a result of the two aims just mentioned, a good scholarly introduction to the sociology of religion in non-western countries. For this investigation, the two world religions of Islam and Buddhism have been singled out − with occasional references to Christianity − as well as Hinduism in India and Judaism in Israel. Altogether seventeen countries are treated, in eight of which Islam is of the various religions the dominating force, whereas Buddhism plays an important role in seven other countries treated.

The research problem at the basis of the book, for which the individual country studies are meant to contribute data, is generally the interaction of religion and society; the way in which this general interaction takes place in the unique historico-cultural context of a given society is the focus of investigation. In the treatment of this basic problem the four religions under consideration are here considered in their interaction with the socio-cultural environments in seventeen countries.

Prices are subject to change without notice

mouton publishers
Berlin · New York · Amsterdam